THE ST. THÉRÈSE OF LISIEUX
PRAYER BOOK

THE
St. Thérèse
of Lisieux
prayer book

BY
VINITA HAMPTON WRIGHT

PARACLETE PRESS
BREWSTER, MASSACHUSETTS

The St. Thérèse of Lisieux Prayer Book

2016 Fourth Printing (POD)
2015 Third Printing
2010 Second Printing
2008 First Printing

Copyright © 2008 by Vinita Hampton Wright

ISBN: 978-1-55725-578-5

All Scripture quotations are taken from the New Revised Standard Version, copyright 1989, 1995 by the Division of Christian Education of the National Council of Churches of Christ in the United States of America. Used by permission. All rights reserved.

Library of Congress Cataloging-in-Publication Data

Wright, Vinita Hampton, 1958-
  The St. Thérèse of Lisieux prayer book / Vinita Hampton Wright.
    p. cm.
  Includes bibliographical references (p.) and indexes.
  ISBN 978-1-55725-578-5
  1. Catholic Church—Prayers and devotions 2. Spiritual life—Catholic Church. 3. Prayer—Catholic Church. 4. Thérèse, de Lisieux, Saint, 1873-1897. I. Title. II. Title: Saint Thérèse of Lisieux prayer book.
  BX2149.2.W755 2008
  242'802–dc22

                                                                2008005076

10 9 8 7 6 5 4

Published by Paraclete Press
Brewster, Massachusetts
www.paracletepress.com
Printed in the United States of America

CONTENTS

III
THE DAILY OFFICE FOR SUNDAY THROUGH SATURDAY
41

IV
PRAYERS AND POEMS OF ST. THÉRÈSE
123

V
SPIRITUAL INFLUENCES IN THE LIFE OF ST. THÉRÈSE

I

THE PRAYER LIFE

of

St. Thérèse of Lisieux

HER CHILDHOOD DEVOTION
AND FAMILY LIFE

*I*f you visit the U.S. National Shrine to St. Thérèse of Lisieux, in Darien, Illinois, and enter the spacious room dedicated to her, one of the first things you'll notice is a collection of portraits on one wall. These are reproductions of photos taken of Thérèse from childhood until just a few months before her death at age twenty-four. Most of these photos are familiar to anyone who has read her autobiography, *The Story of a Soul*, in one of its countless editions, or who has picked up books of her prayers, poems, or letters. Her sister Céline was the photographer in the family, and perhaps because she and Thérèse were closest in age, Céline succeeded in capturing the spirit of her younger sister. She is the child, open-faced and already in love with prayers and piety. She is the adolescent with hair arranged to make her look more grown up—on her way to ask the bishop if she could break rules and tradition to join a convent years before an admissible age. She is a novice, then a fully vowed nun, sober yet content in her work at the Carmelite convent in Lisieux, France. This convent is referred to throughout her story and letters simply as "the Carmel."

In every photograph the eyes reveal a quiet knowing. Here is a person who has figured out very early in life where her heart belongs—with Jesus. Here is a young woman who has made hard choices of the soul before many people have begun even to face their souls in an honest way. Here is person without a college degree who is one of a handful of people in history named "Doctor of the Church."

This series of portraits on the wall provides a short history of Thérèse. In the center of the room, roped off with thick velvet cords, are various artifacts that do the same: a little drum she played as a child, a swatch of blanket from her simple bed in the convent, a tiny piece of her "wedding" dress worn on the day she took her vows, a hand-written note of encouragement to one of the novices she trained, her prayer book, open and displayed in a small glass case. All year long, people come to this room to view the bits and pieces of Thérèse's life. They want to feel a little closer to her. They want to kneel in front of her statue and say *thank you*, or ask for help.

People trust Thérèse. She is young and unlettered and therefore not intimidating in the way St. Augustine might be, or even St. Teresa of Avila, who created a home for Thérèse when she reformed the Carmelite order centuries before Thérèse was born. Thérèse admits, through her writings and her conversations, that because of her youth and various weaknesses of soul, she must thrive spiritually in a "little way" for God. This posture toward the spiritual life is undoubtedly the key to her popularity among millions of people down through the decades. Thérèse discovered, for all of us, that any person can please and love God, through the smallest and most insignificant means. We don't have to be big and important and heroic. We simply have to give God our love, and trust God to love us. This little way to spiritual maturity has opened up a grand thoroughfare for people longing after an authentic experience with God. This is why so many of us wander along those velvet ropes in awe and gratitude, why we gaze at her picture and feel some relief. She was just a child, just a girl, just a young nun with stars in her eyes for Jesus. Here's a person we can walk alongside, a person to whom we can confess our own fears, weaknesses, and immaturity.

Present-day onlookers would likely think of Marie Françoise Thérèse Martin, born January 2, 1873, as an odd child. And if we were to analyze her family life through the lens of twenty-first-century psychology, we would understand immediately that she could never turn out to be anything but a little odd. Both her parents were such devout Catholics that they had each tried, earlier in life, to enter monastic life. Such a life did not work out for either of them, and so they married, had nine children (five of whom survived), and proceeded to create a home filled with prayer, devotion, sanctity, and a spiritual sensibility remarkable even for nineteenth-century France. An early edition of Thérèse's autobiography offers this description in an introductory chapter about her parents:

"O my God"—[Zélie] repeated constantly—"since I am unworthy to be Thy Spouse . . . I shall enter the married state to fulfill Thy Holy Will, and I beseech Thee to make me the mother of many children, and to grant that all of them may be dedicated to Thee." God gave ear to her prayer, and His Finger was visible in the circumstances which led to her becoming the wife of Louis Martin. . . . They were joined together in matrimony—"solely for the love of children, in whom God's Name might be blessed for ever and ever." Nine white flowers bloomed in this sacred garden. Of the nine, four were transplanted to Paradise ere their buds had quite unfolded, while five were gathered in God's walled gardens upon earth, one entering the Visitation Convent at Caen, the others the Carmel of Lisieux.

Thérèse was the baby of the family and, obviously to everyone, the crowning joy of her father.

He called her his little queen, and even into her teen years, she referred to him as her king. Thérèse, along with her four older sisters, enjoyed a comfortable, middle-class life. Mother, father, and girls attended Mass often and prayed daily as a family. Moral and spiritual instruction was woven into the girls' ordinary moments and activities, and early on their mother, Zélie, recognized in their little Thérèse a strong spiritual aptitude. She remarked in a letter: "This poor little one is our happiness, she will be good, you can already see it coming. All she talks about is God; she wouldn't miss saying her prayers for anything."

When Thérèse was only four, Zélie died of breast cancer, and this shattering loss was the first of several that would shape Thérèse's formative years. After her mother's death, the baby of the family claimed the second eldest sister, Pauline, as her new mother, and Pauline took upon herself Thérèse's care, including spiritual formation. Understandably, Thérèse grew extremely attached to Pauline, so much so that when Pauline decided five years later to join the Carmelite Order, nine-year-old Thérèse was so distraught that she became ill. When Pauline left home for life in a cloistered convent, Thérèse clung to the eldest sister, Marie. When, in her twenties, Thérèse would write her autobiography, she would mention numerous times and with great affection how well these sisters had cared for her and helped shape her character and spirituality. Four years after Pauline's departure, Marie followed her to the convent. By this time Thérèse already felt called to become a Carmelite herself. While she remained at home, she took comfort in the constant companionship of Céline, the sister closest to her in age.

As a small child, Thérèse thoroughly enjoyed prayers, the Mass, and devotional practices in general. This love only deepened as she dealt with her mother's death and her sisters' departures from family life. As a young girl she developed a habit of going off by herself, hiding behind a bed or in a closet, to simply think about God the Father, and about Jesus. This sort of spiritual attention is fairly natural to children, something psychologists and experts in faith formation have established in recent times. Thérèse herself realized later that she had been practicing a form of contemplation. And, just as any of us picks up patterns of expression from parents and siblings, her conversations became sprinkled with talk of love and service, sacrifice and humility, all frequent topics of discussion in her household.

It's not surprising that Thérèse did not find companionship outside her own family. She didn't connect with other children at school and seemed to have little interest in events out in "the world" at large. Her own world was small and well-insulated from any culture or viewpoint different from what she experienced at home and church. Because her father and sisters had doted on her, she was for the most part spoiled, self-involved, and hypersensitive—qualities she readily confessed to in her writings, years later. The sensitivity turned out to be a spiritual gift, but for a child bereft of her mother and then two of her favorite sisters-turned-foster-mothers, such tenderness of heart was the source of much pain and distress. Even she understood, as she grew older, that some of her illnesses during that time were in part her own doing, her ability to translate emotional and spiritual distress into severe physical symptoms. What is not so apparent, at first reading of Thérèse's written memories, is that underneath her genuine spiritual appetite and pious language lay a strong will.

During her early adolescence the desire to become a Carmelite nun grew into a strong conviction. She made this known to her sisters and father when she was fourteen. Although Louis Martin was saddened at the prospect of losing one more daughter to the cloister, he respected her wishes and took her to meet with the bishop, because the Superior of Carmel had already made it clear that Thérèse could not enter until age twenty-one. The bishop's decision could alter this. Unfortunately, the bishop was not convinced; perhaps he saw in Thérèse a precious sort of devotion that he feared would prove thin and short-lived when subjected to real life inside the cloister.

Thérèse was not that easily defeated. Soon after this her father took her and Céline on a pilgrimage to Rome, where they had an audience with Pope Leo XIII. Although they, along with the other pilgrims in line, were instructed not to speak to the pontiff, Thérèse knelt before him and asked that, in honor of his jubilee, she be allowed to enter the Carmel at age fifteen. At first he simply told her to do what her superiors told her. The assistants motioned for Thérèse to rise and move on, but she grabbed the pope's knees and said, "Oh, Most Holy Father, if you were to say yes, everyone would be willing!" The Pope looked into her eyes and said, "All right . . . all right. You will enter if it is God's will." Even this did not satisfy the girl completely; the assistants literally had to pick her up and move her away from the pontiff!

That winter, Thérèse learned that she would be allowed to enter the novitiate after Lent. Her fervent prayers had been answered.

PRAYER IN THE CARMELITE CONVENT

It is impossible to understand Thérèse without understanding the Carmelite order she joined at age fifteen, in which she eventually took her final vows, and in which she died at age twenty-four. She would live out her short life in "the Carmel" (as it was called in her conversations and writings) in the town of Lisieux, where her father and remaining sister lived near the family of Zélie's sister and brother-in-law. The spiritual practices of the Carmel fit Thérèse's personality and her family's perceptions of Christian devotion and commitment. The vocabulary used by the Carmelite nuns had been familiar to her from an early age. And her developing ideas about a life calling and an intimacy with God were greatly influenced by life as a Carmelite nun. Some of those ideas seem severe, even unhealthy, to us today. But at that time the Carmelites practiced a form of faith that was considered difficult but well within God's design for a life committed to Christian prayer and service. They lived very simply, in unheated rooms, with few possessions and each nun to a "cell"—a very small room sparsely furnished with a bench and uncomfortable bed. Thérèse and her religious sisters literally prayed for hours each day, did physical labor several hours each day, and fasted regularly—in fact, the reason Thérèse was not allowed to enter the convent at the first of the year was that her older sisters, who were already nuns there, feared that the long fast of the Lenten season would be too severe for a fifteen-year-old girl. Carmelites also practiced self-flagellation—physical whipping for the purpose of disciplining the body—which was not uncommon in religious orders of the day.

The Carmelite order was named for Mt. Carmel of biblical account, where the prophet Elijah faced down the prophets of Baal (1 Kings 18:20–40). During the twelfth century, a group of men lived on the slopes of the mountain range in Palestine known as Carmel, seeking a life of prayer and contemplation. A few decades later, St. Albert, Patriarch of Jerusalem, wrote a rule for them to follow, which was subsequently amended and approved by Pope Innocent IV. This order followed a strict way of life, dedicated to prayer and self-sacrifice. In the thirteenth century, these men left the mountains to live out their devotion elsewhere, and by the fourteenth century they were joined by sister Carmelites of convents in Spain and Italy.

Along with most other religious orders, the Carmelites fell into disarray and corruption during the sixteenth century. In Spain, Carmelite houses were restored largely by the work of St. Teresa of Avila, and the men and women of that order renamed themselves the Discalced Carmelites (*discalced* means "without shoes"—indicating a return to the sort of poverty practiced by the original Carmelites). The writings and teachings of St. Teresa remained influential in the daily life of the Carmel at Lisieux, where great emphasis was placed upon prayer, contemplation, and work.

It was into this way of life little Thérèse, with much ardor and determination, immersed herself. From childhood she had learned, from mother and older sisters especially, that suffering can be a good thing when offered to God for the good of others. Suffering was a major theme in Thérèse's life, and this became even more significant once she had become Jesus' bride. We might wonder about the glory she attributed to suffering and the way she revered the smallest slight or persecution as an opportunity to grow in God's love and favor. But this attitude was in keeping with what people considered Christian piety at that time—and is not so different from Catholic attitudes even in recent decades, about "offering up" our trials and burdens to the Lord. In this context, one aspect of our suffering is that it provides a way for us to be joined with Christ, who suffered for all. In fact, in some mysterious way, we can suffer on behalf of others, taking upon ourselves the sorrow for their sins and interceding for them as we suffer. It's almost as if we are helping Christ to carry the burden of the world's sin, and likewise that we share with Christ in bringing grace to others by submitting in love to our own suffering. This theology of suffering is referenced in the New Testament Epistles that speak of our being in the fellowship of Christ's sufferings, or of being partakers in Christ's suffering.

As to prayer, Thérèse found both fruitfulness and frustration at the Carmel. She deepened her private prayer and meditation, taking more and more joy in her time with God, whether before a picture of Jesus' suffering face, or in Jesus' presence in the Eucharist, or in the silence and loneliness of her cell. What frustrated her—or, rather, what brought out frustration with herself—was the communal prayer, the praying of the offices. Christopher O'Donnell describes a typical day of prayer at the Carmel:

> In Thérèse's time, the Office was spread throughout the day. But the time at which the parts were said no longer reflected the original meaning of each part. In winter the sisters rose at 5:45 AM, and, after an hour of silent prayer, said all the small hours—Prime, Terce, Sext, and None. Vespers were said at 2 PM and Compline at 7:40 PM. Matins and Lauds, which took between 75 and 100 minutes, were said at 9 PM. (In Summer the nuns rose an hour earlier, and everything was advanced by sixty minutes to allow for a siesta or rest period at 1 PM.)

This prayer schedule would be daunting for anyone, but keep in mind that the offices were chanted or sung in Latin. So it's not surprising that Thérèse wished she could connect better with the

Divine Office. She sometimes fell asleep during community prayer. She was obedient to the prayers around the clock, but it seems that her best prayer was in silence, isolation, and contemplation.

MENTAL PRAYER

In being attracted to solitude and prayerful meditation, Thérèse was following in the footsteps of her founding Carmelite saint, St. Teresa of Avila. The great reformer of the order had not only brought its religious back to a lifestyle of true poverty, work, and prayer but had, along with fellow Carmelite St. John of the Cross, further developed the concept of mental prayer.

Teresa and John were both what we would call natural mystics. They used vocal prayer—that is, prayers of the regular liturgies and of the Divine Hours—but much of their most profound spiritual formation and communion with God happened during times of silence, solitude, meditation, and deeper contemplation. Their writings, with which young Thérèse was quite familiar as a Carmelite, testified to the kind of union with God that happened when a person was alone and focused simply upon God's presence.

Thérèse was also a natural for mental prayer. In fact, traditional modes of prayer were often difficult for her.

"I feel then that the fervor of my sisters makes up for my lack of fervor; but when alone (I am ashamed to admit it), the recitation of the rosary is more difficult for me than the wearing of an instrument of penance. . . . I force myself in vain to meditate on the mysteries of the rosary; I don't succeed in fixing my mind on them. . . ." When she felt so arid that it was "impossible to draw forth one single thought to unite me with God, I *very slowly* recite an 'Our Father.'" Though no more conscious of what was occurring than she had been conscious of praying in the old days [as a child] when she sat behind her bed and thought about God, Thérèse's difficulty with conventional forms signaled, according to the teaching of John of the Cross, the call to contemplation.

Not only did Thérèse have trouble with vocal prayers, she didn't take easily to spiritual direction either. She was willing, but with the exception of one priest she had known briefly, but who subsequently moved away, she had difficulty connecting spiritually to a confessor:

I went to confession only a few times, and never spoke about my interior sentiments. The way I was walking was so straight, so clear, I needed no other guide but Jesus. I compared directors to faithful mirrors, reflecting Jesus in souls, and I said that for me God was using no intermediary, he was acting directly!

For Thérèse, as with most mystics, her spiritual nature tended toward solitude and a fellowship with the Divine that was as profound as it was uncomplicated.

Still, contemplation was not merely a matter of sitting around and allowing thoughts of God to float to the surface. Often a person would use an image to focus upon—for Thérèse it was some-times a picture of the Holy Face of Jesus. Sometimes she used a prayer such as the "Our Father." Thérèse mentioned that this was at least a beginning point.

But what most commonly informed Thérèse's long hours of mental prayer were the Scriptures, and more specifically, the Gospels. This aspect of her life is discussed later, but it's important to con-nect it here with the mental prayer she practiced. Without the Gospels—without God's revelation as a foundation—any sort of contemplation would have been meaningless to Thérèse—as it would have been to Mother Teresa of Avila, whose own words were a regular part of the young nun's life.

For Teresa of Avila, St. John of the Cross, Thérèse of Lisieux, and others, mental prayer has served as a powerful spiritual discipline for placing themselves in God's presence with few, if any, outer trappings. Most mystics don't seek this kind of relationship; rather, it is their most honest and natural mode of being with their God.

LOVING JESUS

When Thérèse took her final vows as a Carmelite nun, she wore a wedding dress and veil. Women in religious orders at that time took quite literally their role as brides of Christ. They used love language to describe their relationship with him. However we view this today—as perhaps repressed or at least sublimated sexuality—when Thérèse took the veil, she was choosing what to many was an option preferable to marriage. After all, marriages were often arranged or at least entered into for primarily financial, political, or pragmatic reasons. And once married, a woman could count on having children fairly continuously and, subsequently, might expect to die young from childbirth or complications surrounding it. A married woman was not her own person but more or less the property of her husband. She was expected to serve and obey him and to act in a way publicly that would bring honor to the family. If she belonged to the middle or upper class, she had some opportunities for education, but responsibilities to husband and children trumped all other dreams or desires.

Little wonder that so many young women chose marriage to Jesus rather than to another human. Jesus would not burden them with sexual demands and multiple pregnancies. Jesus' love would always be perfect, never cruel and oppressive, as human love could sometimes be. And, in their union with Jesus, they could bring God's love to others on a much grander scale. Rather than tending to the spiritual lives of their own offspring, they would pray night and day for the whole world. They would offer their hard beds, unheated rooms, rigorous schedules, and long loneliness for the salvation of others.

Thérèse had loved Jesus since earliest childhood. For her, entrance into the Carmelite way simply allowed her to love Jesus more completely and without worldly distractions. She never appeared to be interested in traditional marriage. And although life in the convent was hard, she claimed that it was what she had imagined—no unpleasant surprises. Unfortunately, she didn't connect with the community of sisters and her Mother Superior much better than she had with her classmates years before. She continued to be the odd one, the youngest person in the room whose enthusiasm for faith seemed a little too good to be true and whose fervent spiritual practice sometimes made others uncomfortable.

Given her history—middle-class childhood, high sensitivity and emotional neediness, a series of deep hurts and disappointments—we might expect that life in the convent would only push Thérèse into emotional shutdown or worse. (Her father suffered an episode of mental illness not quite a year after Thérèse left home for the Carmel.) However, Thérèse—despite her childishness and naiveté— truly was called by God to serve as a Carmelite. As time passed, she was able to take hold of her own soul and allow Jesus' love and the Holy Spirit's power to use her hurt to shape and discipline her. She took upon herself the practice of what she termed the "Little Way," giving herself completely to the ordinary details of life because, she reasoned, she would never be a spiritual giant (After all, she kept sleeping through prayers!).

When she contracted tuberculosis at age twenty-three, she received the diagnosis as a final calling to suffer for Jesus, to somehow accomplish through her own hardship the holy work of the world's salvation, continuing the work Jesus' suffering had begun.

It took her roughly fourteen months to die, and during that time, at the Mother Superior's request, Thérèse continued a task she had begun a few years earlier: writing the story of her life and of her soul's development. At that time she was also training novices, becoming for them a sort of spiritual director. That she was given this responsibility is evidence that the Mother Superior recognized in this young girl a spiritual acuity that must be honored and tended.

Thérèse offered spiritual prayer and companionship to two missionary priests, writing careful letters to one of them until she was but a few days from death. She also wrote various letters, mostly to family members. During her final weeks, her sisters took note of practically everything she said.

Her death was excruciating, unaided by morphine because her Superior believed that the suffering itself was part and parcel of the calling to die for her Lord.

After Thérèse died, her autobiography was sent around the circuit of convents, which was the custom. Soon people were responding to this young life-in-words, first in the convents but soon far beyond. The ripples caused by this young woman's fervent and straightforward spirituality just kept multiplying, as described here by biographer Patricia O'Connor:

By 1905, eight years after Thérèse's death, *The Story of a Soul* had been translated into English, Polish, Italian, Spanish, Dutch, Portuguese, German, Japanese, and Russian. The letters kept coming and so did the pilgrims, many of them priests. And so did young women eager to be Carmelites like Thérèse. They came from France, Ireland,

Italy, Portugal, even Istanbul—too many for the small monastery to hold.

Thérèse was beatified in 1923, and in 1925, at a ceremony in Rome, held in St. Peter's Basilica, she was declared a saint. More than 60,000 people gathered in the church for this special occasion. Outside, the crowd numbered well over 200,000— as reported by a correspondent for *The New York Times*. Just a few decades later, in 1997, Pope John Paul II declared Thérèse of Lisieux a Doctor of the Church.

She was the "Little Flower," who bloomed but a few years on earth, in one small convent in France. Yet she continues to be one of the most popular saints of the global Church. Perhaps people needed a new example of what glory really looks like in God's kingdom—full of humility and bright with simply love for the Divine.

II
PRAYING ALONGSIDE
St. Thérèse

AN INTRODUCTION

FOLLOWING IS A WEEK of morning and evening prayer based upon themes that emerge in the life of St. Thérèse of Lisieux. These prayers come from a combination of sources that would have been meaningful to Thérèse. The liturgical prayer she performed at the convent would be difficult to reproduce here; most of it was in Latin, and she herself did not understand it word by word. However, some portions of the communal evening prayer were read in French. Included in this liturgy are some of the standard prayers and psalms used at that time for morning and evening prayer.

Thérèse grew up praying from a multivolume book called *The Liturgical Year*, a book her father used faithfully for daily family prayer time. This source was used sometimes in the convent as well. Some of those prayers are also included in this liturgy.

Because we have the amazing record of Thérèse's life and thought, through her autobiography, as well as through many of her letters and poems, we are able to use numerous Scripture references that she cited; thus we can meditate on Scriptures that were especially meaningful to her.

Morning and evening offices in the convent each took close to an hour and a half, with multiple psalms and other readings. This liturgy is shortened and somewhat simplified, in order to help you participate in a prayer experience similar to Thérèse's while also engaging with her through her own reflections.

The sequence for each day of liturgy is as follows:

A. QUOTE OF ST. THÉRÈSE

B. PREPARATION: simple prayer of intention

C. GOSPEL SENTENCE: a brief yet powerful introduction to the day's topic

D. SILENCE: for a minute or more

E. CONFESSION: in the morning, a penitential psalm; in the evening, one of the various standard confessions

F. FIRST READING: from the Hebrew prophets or New Testament Epistles

G. PSALM

H. GOSPEL READING

I. SILENCE

J. PRAYERS OF THE SAINTS: ones that Thérèse may have prayed or that were written by early Carmelites

K. PRAYER FOR THE DAY or PRAYER FOR NIGHT-TIME: using various prayers of the time

These prayer liturgies can be used in a variety of ways. If you already practice morning and evening prayer, you can substitute these prayers for a week of your ordinary readings. Or you might add these prayers to those already in your schedule, to enhance a particular week of your prayer time.

These prayers might also serve as a separate retreat with Thérèse, practiced over a week as suggested or used in a shorter time span, concentrated into two or three days of prayer focused on the themes of Thérèse.

These liturgies can be prayed alone or used in a group. If they are prayed in a group, specific readings can be assigned to different people, and the psalms can be read responsively—that is, half the group reading one verse, and the other half reading the next, for the duration of the psalm.

We come to know God in our time alone with God. We also come to know God in community. This book offers a unique opportunity to spend time with God, in the company of Thérèse of Lisieux. As you pray to God, you can enjoy the sense that these prayers were part of Thérèse's journey of faith. You may feel comfortable inviting Thérèse to pray them again alongside you. Her presence can become more real to you as you dwell on her own words that are included in the liturgies. Together, you can continue upon your "little way" of loving God and enjoying God's love for you.

While we envision these prayers in the hands of individuals as they enrich their personal devotions, this book might also serve groups of people devoted to St. Thérèse, whether lay prayer partners or academic colleagues. Our hope is that these themes, prayers, and Thérèse's words will assist you in understanding not only the "little flower" who was Thérèse the Carmelite nun but also your own life calling, and the next step in your vocation, whatever it may be.

THEMES FOR SEVEN DAYS OF PRAYER

Thérèse lived out various spiritual themes, but we have chosen only seven, one to serve as a framework for each day of prayer. With few exceptions, all Scripture passages used here were cited in Thérèse's own writings. And many of the prayers most likely were prayed by her Carmelite community.

Day One—Abandonment to Love

It's safe to say that Thérèse's family—and later, her family of sisters in the convent—saw her as fragile. Her early illnesses and sensitive emotional life marked her as someone who must be cared for. Members of her extended family didn't think her very smart or functional, and other Carmelite sisters had low expectations of this pious and pampered teenager who had entered their midst.

Thérèse herself seemed to understand that her own abilities would never be sufficient for the saintly life she wanted to live. So she fixed her sight on God's love, and that love alone, for everything she was to become. She turned to that love when circumstances were challenging and when her own faith was flagging. We can take comfort in knowing that Therese did not consider herself very good at prayer or holy living. Her maturity grew out of her ever-sharpening realization that by herself she would never attain spiritual perfection. We, too, can develop the habit of facing our inadequacies and using them to compel us more fully and automatically into reliance upon God's all-enveloping love.

"Offer to God a sacrifice of praise and thanksgiving" (cf. Psalm 50:14, cf. Hebrews 13:15). This, then, is what Jesus requires of us. He has no need of our works, but only of our love, for this same God who declares that He has no need to tell us if He is hungry, was not afraid to beg for a little water from the Samaritan woman. He was thirsty. . . . But in saying, "Give me a drink" (John 4:7), it was the love of His poor creature that the Creator of the universe was asking for. He was thirsty for love. . . . Oh! I feel more than ever that Jesus is thirsty. He meets only ungrateful and indifferent people among the disciples of the world, and among his own disciples, He finds, alas! Few hearts that give themselves to Him without reserve, who understand all the tenderness of His infinite Love.

—autobiography: Edmonson, 209

Day Two—Prayer of the Heart

Thérèse was brought up in a household that prayed, and when she entered Carmel, she took upon herself a rigorous daily schedule of prayer. But the prayers that worked on her soul the most were her honest and spontaneous responses to Jesus her Beloved, to Mary her Holy Mother, and to God her heavenly Father. Some of these prayers also made an immediate impact on the people who read her autobiography and who were the recipients of her personal letters. There was a directness to these prayers, a simplicity and trust, that revealed a relentless love for God and a desire for God to respond to her.

Sometimes we advance the most in our spiritual life when we become tired of trying so hard to practice spirituality on other people's terms. We try to pray as this person does, or to talk about the spiritual life as that person expresses it. After awhile we give up those efforts and simply talk to God in our words and our own way. Thérèse made this transition early on.

> The power of prayer is really tremendous. It makes one like a queen who can approach the king at any time and get whatever she asks for. To be sure of an answer, there is no need to recite from a book a formula composed for the occasion. If there were, I should have to be pitied.
>
> Though I'm quite unworthy, I love to say the Divine Office every day, but apart from that I cannot bring myself to hunt through books for beautiful prayers. There are so many of them that I get a headache. Besides, each prayer seems lovelier than the next. I cannot possibly say them all and do not know which to choose, I behave like children who cannot read: I tell God very simply what I want and He always understands.
>
> —autobiography: Beevers, 139

Day Three—Sensitivity of Spirit

Although Thérèse's spiritual sensitivity awakened an early love for God, at times it made life more difficult for her. For one thing, not many people understood her spiritual fervor and attention. For another, she had to carry that sensitivity through the normal phases of childhood and adolescence, which brought along their particular upheavals of spirit and emotion. Undoubtedly, the early loss of her mother, and the subsequent losses of her older sisters who left home for the convent, tenderized her heart even more to pain and anxiety.

A spiritually sensitive person notices details other people don't notice. She is more easily bothered by ordinary ups and downs that many of us simply gloss over or ignore. While most people shake their heads over sin and evil, a person like Thérèse is devastated by the same.

How many of us have been accused of being too sensitive, in one way or another? Sometimes we are overly vulnerable to getting our feelings hurt, or we are too quick to take offense. But usually that sensitivity radiates further out into life. For instance, we are more likely to be upset about injustice and wrongdoing in society as a whole. Of course, we are encouraged to "leave well enough alone" rather than stir up trouble. If we speak up about sinful activities that hurt others, we are labeled fanatics. Perhaps we refuse to go to movies that are violent because we know that it has a real impact on our spirit, or we abstain from joining in workplace gossip because we don't consider silly gossip to be harmless.

Spiritual sensitivity causes us to be bothered easily by anything that isn't right and holy, whether it's news we read in the paper or the way another person talks to us in a given situation.

Left to itself, this kind of attention to daily occurrences and feelings can lead to emotional suffering, neuroses, and even mental illness. But when faithfully and prayerfully nurtured, that same sensitivity can be channeled into astute spiritual attention to the moment at hand and to whatever presents itself in people and events.

Ultimately, the person who is spiritually sensitive must make a choice. Will she be tossed about by each and every thing, or will she learn to detach herself from her own deep reactions in order to be moved by God's Spirit in response to the situation? This was the course that Thérèse took, and she became a master of detachment. Whereas at one time everything had mattered to her to the extreme, she reached a point of saying, "I'm suffering very much, but am I suffering very well? That's the point!"

—The Yellow Notebook: August 18, #1

Day Four—Suffering with Faith

Suffering was a hallmark of Catholic piety in nineteenth-century France. Thérèse had been instructed about the virtue of suffering from the time she was little. Life in the Carmel treated suffering as something of a spiritual discipline. It was not uncommon for Christians of that time to romanticize the idea of martyrdom and even hope for the opportunity to suffer in glorious ways for God's kingdom. (This tendency was due partly to a strong antireligion attitude prevailing in French culture outside the church.) In her autobiography, Thérèse makes various references to her early fantasies about martyrdom. She and her sisters had dreamed of dying horrible deaths for their Lord and Savior.

By the time Thérèse embarked upon her personal journey of hard suffering—her contracting tuberculosis at age twenty-three—her ideas about martyrdom had changed. She understood that, like everything else, the glory was not in the suffering so much as it was in a person's trust in God's love, whatever form that suffering took. This is one of the hallmarks of her spirituality for us, that we, too, might learn to see our own, perhaps smaller sufferings, as part of God's plan for our lives. She who had dreamed of glorious public martyrdom would die a long, painful, and fairly private death in bed within the cloister of the Carmel.

Thérèse's illness was so protracted that at times she concluded she would not die for Jesus but simply keep on living in horrible pain and constant suffocation. It would have been much easier to die—could she offer to God her *inability* to die? Could she keep trusting in her Bridegroom when it seemed he would never show up to claim her?

We who run in the way of love shouldn't be thinking of sufferings that can take place in the future; it's a lack of confidence, it's like meddling in the work of creation.

—The Yellow Notebook: July 23, #3

Since my First Communion, since the time I asked Jesus to change all the consolations of this earth into bitterness for me, I had a perpetual desire to suffer. I wasn't thinking, however, of making suffering my joy; this is a grace that was given to me later on. Up until then, it was like a spark hidden beneath the ashes, and like blossoms on a tree that must become fruit in time.

—The Yellow Notebook: July 31, #13

Day Five—Trust in God's Grace

Truly trusting in God is rarely easy for any of us. So much gets in the way: others' unfair or hostile treatment, unbearable circumstances, our own unhealthy emotional habits, and the spiritual dark night of the soul, during which we lose all sense of God's presence. Thérèse suffered her own dark night—something she understood at least partially because she was well-versed in the writings of St. John of the Cross, who had coined that term and written extensively about the dark night.

During these times, when it seemed that God had abandoned her, Thérèse's strong will—

something her family had recognized in her since childhood—served her in a positive way. She simply would not give up on Jesus. She decided at different times that he was casting her off like an unwanted toy. She wasn't always happy about his response, or lack of response, to her. Yet, she had devoted herself to be a bride of Christ, and she refused to let go or turn back.

Quite frankly, she held God to God's word. God was trustworthy and faithful—she cited many Scriptures about this—and so she would keep on trusting, no matter what happened.

> I was treating [Jesus] as a child would who thinks it can do what it likes, looking upon its father's treasures as its own.
>
> —autobiography: Day, 101

Day Six—Humility in All Things

Life in the Carmelite convent could be trying in a lot of ways. The life itself was not easy—highly structured and focusing on service and self-deprivation. Add to that various sisters with their little idiosyncrasies and not-so-little faults, and daily life could become an endurance test. Thérèse's Mother Superior apparently decided to root out of this young, somewhat spoiled girl any expectations of special treatment. From Thérèse's writings we know that she hungered for the older woman's attention, but to no avail.

Thérèse understood eventually that this harshness had been what she needed. Still, the girl's humiliations were many, even from her first days of convent life. Other nuns caused her suffering as well; one served her the worst food at meals; another, who was elderly and quite feeble, accepted Thérèse's daily assistance but abused her for it.

When a person lived in a closed community, the details could become more and more irritating: someone clicking her teeth in chapel, another snatching your pitcher and replacing it with a chipped one. So Thérèse determined that she must make humility her goal at all times and in all situations. It was almost as if she took the offensive. She chose close proximity to the nun she liked the least. When a visitor rang the doorbell—providing an opportunity to have contact with the outside world—Thérèse moved slowly enough that another nun could enjoy the privilege. As the years went by, she turned small challenges into opportunities to share in Christ's humility.

It has been said that we can know how much of a servant of God we are by how we react when someone actually treats us like a servant. Thérèse recognized the truth of this; if she resisted the situations in which others treated her poorly, what did that really say about her willingness to be used by God however God chose?

Every day, each of us is presented with opportunity to react not as a proud person trying to be significant, but as a humble child of God who is already significant because of God's favor and love.

> If it happens to me to think and to say something that pleases my Sisters, I find it quite natural for them to take it over as belonging to themselves. That thought belongs to the Holy Spirit and not to me, since St. Paul said that without the Spirit of Love we can't give the name "Father" to our Father who is in heaven. So He's quite free to use me to give a good thought to a soul. If I believed that thought belongs to me, I would be like "the donkey bearing relics" who thought that the homage being paid to the Saints was addressed to him.
>
> —autobiography: Edmonson, 263

Day Seven—*Living by the Little Way*

Catholics and others the world over have come to know "The Little Way" as the spiritual path of St. Thérèse of Lisieux. The young girl seemed to understand that she would never become a great scholar or have much stature at all within the walls of Carmel. She had trouble with formal prayer. She was too young and inexperienced to do "big" things or even make a big difference. All she knew was that, from an early age, she had wanted to become one of God's saints. She felt that this was her calling, to be a bride of Jesus and to help souls throughout the world through her personal suffering and her prayers.

Possibly because she received little esteem from her own Carmelite community, Thérèse pondered her situation and then devised a way to live as a saint.

> I've told myself: God wouldn't know how to inspire desires that can't be realized. So despite my littleness I can aspire to sainthood. To make myself bigger is impossible; I have to put up with myself such as I am with all my imperfections. But I want to seek the means of going to heaven by a little way that is very straight, very short, a completely new little way.
>
> —autobiography: Edmonson, 230

She would simply live God's love in the littlest details. Everything she did would be in service to her Jesus. This is the aspect of Thérèse's spirituality that is most treasured—and perhaps least imitated—by those of us who read her today. Still, we can begin this day to offer the next moment, the next word, feeling, or problem, to Jesus. Then we can practice confidence that, whatever we are too little to accomplish, God will certainly do. Not only that, God will somehow include us in the doing.

III

The Daily Office

FOR SUNDAY THROUGH SATURDAY

MORNING PRAYER
Sunday
Theme: Abandonment to Love

FROM THÉRÈSE

How sweet is the way of love! Of course one may stumble and be guilty of small faults, but love, able to draw good from everything, will very quickly destroy all that displeases Jesus and will fill one's heart with a deep and humble peace.

PREPARATION

Lord Jesus, you abandoned Heaven itself
in order to be with us,
to love us with healing touch
and discerning gaze.
You gave yourself to each day,
offering the gift of your presence
to those who sought you.
Help us to be so free with ourselves
that we offer our whole presence to this day
and to your unbounded love.

GOSPEL SENTENCE

VERY TRULY, I TELL YOU, unless a grain of wheat falls into the earth and dies, it remains just a single grain; but if it dies, it bears much fruit. Those who love their life lose it, and those who hate their life in this world will keep it for eternal life.

—John 12:24–25

SILENCE

PENITENTIAL PSALM
Psalm 6

O LORD, do not rebuke me in your anger,
    or discipline me in your wrath.
Be gracious to me, O LORD, for I am languishing;
O LORD, heal me, for my bones are shaking
    with terror.
My soul also is struck with terror,
    while you, O LORD—how long?

Turn, O LORD, save my life;
    deliver me for the sake of your steadfast love.
For in death there is no remembrance of you;
    in Sheol who can give you praise?

I am weary with my moaning;
    every night I flood my bed with tears;

I drench my couch with my weeping.
My eyes waste away because of grief;
　　they grow weak because of all my foes.

Depart from me, all you workers of evil,
　　for the LORD has heard the sound of my
　　weeping.
The LORD has heard my supplication;
　　the LORD accepts my prayer.
All my enemies shall be ashamed
　　and struck with terror;
　　they shall turn back, and in a moment be put
　　to shame.

FIRST READING

Draw me after you, let us make haste.
　　The king has brought me into his chambers.
We will exult and rejoice in you;
　　we will extol your love more than wine;
　　rightly do they love you.
. . .
With great delight I sat in his shadow,
　　and his fruit was sweet to my taste.
He brought me to the banqueting house,
　　　　and his intention toward me was love.
　　　　　　　　　—Song of Solomon 1:4; 2:3a–4

45

The LORD is merciful and gracious,
  slow to anger and abounding in steadfast love.
He will not always accuse,
  nor will he keep his anger for ever.
He does not deal with us according to our sins,
  nor repay us according to our iniquities.
For as the heavens are high above the earth,
  so great is his steadfast love
  towards those who fear him;
as far as the east is from the west,
  so far he removes our transgression from us.
As a father has compassion for his children,
  so the LORD has compassion for those who
  fear him.
For he knows how we were made;
  he remembers that we are dust.

GOSPEL READING

NO ONE HAS ASCENDED INTO HEAVEN except the
one who descended from heaven, the Son of
Man. And just as Moses lifted up the serpent in
the wilderness, so must the Son of Man be lifted
up, that whoever believes in him may have eternal
life. For God so loved the world that he gave his
only Son, so that everyone who believes in him
may not perish but may have eternal life. Indeed,
God did not send the Son into the world to

condemn the world, but in order that the world might be saved through him.

—John 3:13–17

SILENCE

PRAYERS OF THE SAINTS

May I recall all of these graces, especially when I come to adore you in your sanctuary, or when I offer you my soul for your residence! I will say a thousand times, "Come, divine Jesus. Accept this heart that you have desired to closely unite with. Would that my heart would be all for you, that it would not look for any other love than yours, that it would have no life other than yours. With an attentive, generous, faithful love, may I respond always to your love in honor of your first visit."

—Venerable Mother Therese of St. Augustine

PRAYER FOR THE DAY

O Jesus! thou Sun of the world's salvation! shine in the depth of our souls; for now is the hour of night's departure, and sweeter daybreak dawns upon the earth.

O thou that givest us this acceptable time! give us to wash, with our tears, the victim we offer thee, which is our heart; and grant that it may burn with joyous love.

If the rod of penance but strike these hearts of stone, a flood of ceaseless tears will flow from that same fount, whence came our many sins.

The day, thine own day, is at hand, when all things bloom afresh; oh! grant that we, too, may rejoice, being brought once more to the path, by thy right hand.

O merciful Trinity! may the world prostrate itself before thee, and adore; and we, made new by grace, sing a new canticle of praise. Amen.

—Early Lenten hymn

Sunday

FROM THÉRÈSE

"He shall gather together the lambs with His arm, and shall take them up into His bosom" (Isaiah 40:11). As if all this were not proof enough, the same prophet, piercing the depths of eternity with eyes inspired, cried out in the name of Our Lord: "You shall be carried at the breasts, and upon the knees they shall caress you. As one whom the mother caresseth, so will I comfort you" (Isaiah 66:12–13a). . . . One can only remain silent, one can only weep for gratitude and love, after words like these.

PREPARATION

We have done with this day what we have done.
We cannot change the hours past
but only offer them to you, God.
Every imperfection, every matter incomplete,
every failure of spirit and every effort at love
we leave within the heart of
your all-consuming love.

You are over all and in all,
and no matter what we have done
or failed to do, you are enough.

GOSPEL SENTENCE

THERE WAS ALSO A PROPHET, Anna . . . a widow to
the age of eighty-four. She never left the temple
but worshiped there with fasting and prayer night
and day.   Luke 2:36–37

SILENCE

CONFESSION

I confess to almighty God, to blessed Mary ever-
Virgin, to blessed Michael the Archangel, to
blessed John the Baptist, to the holy apostles Peter
and Paul, and to all the saints, that I have sinned
exceedingly in thought, word, and deed; through
my fault, through my most grievous fault.
Therefore I beseech the blessed Mary ever-Virgin,
blessed Michael the Archangel, blessed John the
Baptist, the holy apostles Peter and Paul, and all
the saints, to pray to the Lord our God for me.

May almighty God have mercy on us, and
our sins being forgiven, bring us to life everlasting. Amen.

For thus says the Lord:
I will extend prosperity to her like a river,
and the wealth of the nations like an overflowing
    stream;
and you shall nurse and be carried on her arm,
and dandled on her knees.
As a mother comforts her child,
so I will comfort you;
you shall be comforted in Jerusalem.
You shall see, and your heart shall rejoice;
your bodies shall flourish like the grass;
and it shall be known that the hand of the Lord
    is with his servants,
and his indignation is against his enemies.

—Isaiah 66:12–14

PSALM 50:12–15

If I were hungry, I would not tell you,
    for the world and all that is in it is mine.
Do I eat the flesh of bulls,
    or drink the blood of goats?
Offer to God a sacrifice of thanksgiving,
    and pay your vows to the Most High.
Call on me in the day of trouble;
    I will deliver you, and you shall glorify me.

THEREFORE I TELL YOU, do not worry about your life, what you will eat or what you will drink, or about your body, what you will wear. Is not life more than food, and the body more than clothing? Look at the birds of the air; they neither sow nor reap nor gather into barns, and yet your heavenly Father feeds them. Are you not of more value than they? . . .

But if God so clothes the grass of the field, which is alive today and tomorrow is thrown into the oven, will he not much more clothe you—you of little faith? Therefore do not worry, saying, "What will we eat?" or "What will we drink?" or "What will we wear?" For . . . your heavenly Father knows that you need all these things. But strive first for the kingdom of God and his righteousness, and all these things will be given to you as well.

—Matthew 6:25–26, 30–33

SILENCE

PRAYERS OF THE SAINTS

In order that my life may be one Act of perfect Love, I offer myself as a Victim of Holocaust to Thy Merciful Love, imploring Thee to consume me unceasingly, and to allow the floods of infinite tenderness gathered up to Thee to overflow into my soul, that so I may become a very martyr of Thy Love, O my God! May this martyrdom, after having prepared me to appear in Thy Presence, free me from this life at the last, and may my soul take its flight—without delay—into the eternal embrace of Thy Merciful Love!

—St. Thérèse of Lisieux

PRAYER FOR NIGHTTIME

O God! who has enlightened the most sacred of nights by the brightness of him who is the true Light; grant that we who have known the mysteries of this Light on earth may likewise come to the enjoyment of it in heaven. Amen.

Monday

Theme: Prayer of the Heart

FROM THÉRÈSE

I used to go into a space there was behind my bed which I could shut off with the bed curtain. And there I used to think . . . about God, about life . . . about eternity. . . . . I realize now that I was engaged in mental prayer without knowing it and that God was teaching me it in secret.

PREPARATION

Lord Jesus, help us speak clearly to you;
You know our hearts, so why should we
say anything but what is true?
Help us know our own desires, fears,
our anger as well as our brightest dreams.
May this prayer be a loving conversation
between us.

I TELL YOU, there will be more joy in heaven over one sinner who repents than over ninety-nine righteous persons who need no repentance.

—Luke 15:7

SILENCE

PENITENTIAL PSALM
Psalm 32

Happy are those whose transgression is forgiven,
    whose sin is covered.
Happy are those to whom the LORD imputes no
    iniquity,
and in whose spirit there is no deceit.

While I kept silence, my body wasted away
    through my groaning all day long.
For day and night your hand was heavy upon me;
    my strength was dried up as by the heat of
    summer.

Then I acknowledged my sin to you,
    and I did not hide my iniquity;
I said, "I will confess my transgressions to the
    LORD,"
    and you forgave the guilt of my sin.

Therefore let all who are faithful offer prayer to
   you;
      at a time of distress, the rush of mighty waters
      shall not reach them.
You are a hiding place for me;
   you preserve me from trouble;
you surround me with glad cries of deliverance.

I will instruct you and teach you the way you
   should go;
      I will counsel you with my eye upon you.
Do not be like a horse or a mule,
   without understanding,
      whose temper must be curbed with bit and
      bridle,
      else it will not stay near you.

Many are the torments of the wicked,
   but steadfast love surrounds those who trust in
   the LORD.
Be glad in the LORD and rejoice, O righteous,
   and shout for joy, all you upright in heart.

FIRST READING

But with me it is a very small thing that I should
be judged by you or by any human court. I do not
even judge myself. . . . It is the Lord who judges
me. Therefore do not pronounce judgment

before the time, before the Lord comes, who will bring to light the things now hidden in darkness and will disclose the purposes of the heart. Then each one will receive commendation from God.

—1 Corinthians 4:3–5

PSALM 139:1–4

O LORD, you have searched me and known me.
You know when I sit down and when I rise up;
   you discern my thoughts from far away.
You search out my path and my lying down,
   and are acquainted with all my ways.
Even before a word is on my tongue,
   O LORD, you know it completely.

GOSPEL READING

AND WHENEVER YOU PRAY, do not be like the hypocrites; for they love to stand and pray in the synagogues and at the street corners, so that they may be seen by others. Truly I tell you, they have received their reward. But whenever you pray, go into your room and shut the door and pray to your Father who is in secret; and your Father who sees in secret will reward you.

When you are praying, do not heap up empty phrases as the Gentiles do; for they think that they will be heard because of their many words. Do not be like them, for your Father knows what you need before you ask him.

—Matthew 6:5–8

SILENCE

PRAYERS OF THE SAINTS

How good and how sweet it is, Jesus, to dwell in your heart! All my thoughts and affections will I sink in the Heart of Jesus, my Lord. I have found the Heart of my king, my brother, my friend, the Heart of my beloved Jesus. And now that I have found your Heart, which is also mine, dear Jesus, I will pray to you. Grant that my prayer may reach you, may find entrance to your Heart. Draw me to yourself. O Jesus, who are infinitely above all beauty and every charm, wash me clean from my defilement; wipe out even the smallest trace of sin. If you, who are all-pure, will purify me, I will be able to make my way into your Heart and dwell there all my life long. There I will learn to know your will, and find the grace to fulfill it. Amen.

—St. Bernard of Clairvaux

O God, who makes the souls of the faithful to be of one will, grant unto your people to love what you command, and desire what you promise, that in a world of change our hearts may there be fixed where true joys abide. Through Jesus Christ, your Son our Lord, who lives and reigns with you in the unity of the Holy Spirit, God world without end. Amen.

EVENING PRAYER
Monday

Theme: Prayer of the Heart

FROM THÉRÈSE

For me, prayer is an upward rising of the heart, it's a simple glance toward heaven, it's a cry of gratitude and love in the midst of trials as much as in the midst of joys. In short, it's something big, something great, something supernatural that expands my heart and unites me to Jesus.

PREPARATION

Lord God, may we approach you
with honesty of spirit and humility of heart.
May we always understand to our depths
that you are Lord over all
and that you have created us;
that we exist and thrive because
you have chosen to love us,
to speak with us, to teach us mysteries
and fill us with your joy.

GOSPEL SENTENCE

BUT [HE] WOULD NOT EVEN LOOK UP to heaven, but was beating his breast and saying, "God, be merciful to me, a sinner!" I tell you, this man went down to his home justified . . . for all who exalt themselves will be humbled, but all who humble themselves will be exalted.

—Luke 18:13–14

SILENCE

CONFESSION

O my God, I am exceedingly grieved for having offended thee, and with my whole heart I repent of the sins I have committed. I hate and abhor them above every other evil, not only because, by so sinning, I have lost heaven and deserve hell, but still more because I have offended thee, O infinite Goodness, who art worthy to be loved above all things. I most firmly resolve, by the assistance of thy grace, never more to offend thee for the time to come, and to avoid those occasions which might lead me into sin.

Then I looked, and there was the Lamb, standing on Mount Zion! And with him were one hundred forty-four thousand who had his name and his Father's name written on their foreheads. And I heard a voice from heaven like the sound of many waters and like the sound of loud thunder; the voice I heard was like the sound of harpists playing on their harps, and they sing a new song before the throne and before the four living creatures and before the elders. No one could learn that song except [those] who have been redeemed from the earth. . . . [T]hese follow the Lamb wherever he goes. They have been redeemed from humankind as first fruits for God and the Lamb, and in their mouth no lie was found; they are blameless.

—Revelation 14:1–5

PSALM 141:1–2

I call upon you, O LORD; come quickly to me;
give ear to my voice when I call to you.
Let my prayer be counted as incense before you,
and the lifting up of my hands as an evening
    sacrifice.

. . . [JESUS] LOOKED UP TO HEAVEN and said, "Father, the hour has come; glorify your Son so that the Son may glorify you, since you have given him authority over all people, to give eternal life to all whom you have given him. And this is eternal life; that they may know you, the only true God, and Jesus Christ whom you have sent. I glorified you on earth by finishing the work that you gave me to do. So now, Father, glorify me in your own presence with the glory that I had in your presence before the world existed.

"I have made your name known to those whom you gave me from the world. They were yours, and you gave them to me, and they have kept your word. Now they know that everything you have given me is from you; for the words that you gave to me I have given to them, and they have received them and know in truth that I came from you; and they have believed that you sent me. I am asking on their behalf; I am not asking on behalf of the world, but on behalf of those whom you gave me, because they are yours."

—John 17:1–9

SILENCE

Come, adore this wondrous presence,
Bow to Christ, the source of grace.
Here is kept the ancient promise
Of God's earthly dwelling place.
Sight is blind before God's glory,
Faith alone may see his face.

Glory be to God the Father,
Praise to his co-equal Son,
Adoration to the Spirit,
Bond of love, in Godhead one.
Blest be God by all creation
joyously while endless ages run. Amen.
—St. Thomas Aquinas

PRAYER FOR NIGHTTIME

O almighty and everlasting God, who, by the
cooperation of the Holy Ghost, didst prepare the
body and soul of Mary, glorious Virgin and
Mother, to become the worthy habitation of thy
Son; grant that we may be delivered from present
evils, and from everlasting death by her gracious
intercession, in whose commemoration we
rejoice. Through the same Christ our Lord.
Amen.

MORNING PRAYER

Tuesday

Theme: Sensitivity of Spirit

FROM THÉRÈSE

A heart given to God loses none of its natural tenderness; on the contrary, the more pure and divine it becomes, the more such tenderness increases.

PREPARATION

Dear Lord of All,
Quiet our minds and still our souls.
Open our understanding
that we may hear your voice.
Make our hearts tender enough
to receive your grace.

GOSPEL SENTENCE

MARY TREASURED ALL THESE WORDS and pondered them in her heart.

—Luke 2:19

PENITENTIAL PSALM
Psalm 38

O LORD, do not rebuke me in your anger,
    or discipline me in your wrath.
For your arrows have sunk into me,
    and your hand has come down on me.

There is no soundness in my flesh
    because of your indignation;
there is no health in my bones
    because of my sin.
For my iniquities have gone over my head;
    they weigh like a burden too heavy for me.

My wounds grow foul and fester
    because of my foolishness;
I am utterly bowed down and prostrate;
    all day long I go around mourning.
For my loins are filled with burning,
    and there is no soundness in my flesh.
I am utterly spent and crushed;
    I groan because of the tumult of my heart.

O LORD, all my longing is known to you;
    my sighing is not hidden from you.
My heart throbs, my strength fails me;

as for the light of my eyes—it also has gone
   from me.
My friends and companions stand aloof from
   my affliction,
and my neighbors stand far off.

Those who seek my life lay their snares;
   those who seek to hurt me speak of ruin,
   and meditate treachery all day long.

But I am like the deaf, I do not hear;
   like the mute, who cannot speak.
Truly, I am like one who does not hear,
   and in whose mouth is no retort.

But it is for you, O LORD, that I wait;
   it is you, O LORD my God, who will answer.
For I pray, "Only do not let them rejoice over me,
   those who boast against me when my foot
slips."

For I am ready to fall,
   and my pain is ever with me.
I confess my iniquity;
   I am sorry for my sin.
Those who are my foes without cause are mighty,
   and many are those who hate me wrongfully.
Those who render me evil for good
   are my adversaries because I follow after good.

Do not forsake me, O LORD;
O my God, do not be far from me;
make haste to help me,
O LORD, my salvation.

FIRST READING

Now there was a great wind, so strong that it was
splitting mountains and breaking rocks in pieces
before the Lord, but the Lord was not in the
wind; and after the wind an earthquake, but the
Lord was not in the earthquake, and after the
earthquake a fire, but the Lord was not in the fire;
and after the fire a sound of sheer silence. When
Elijah heard it, he wrapped his face in his mantle
and went out and stood at the entrance of the
cave. Then there came a voice to him that said,
"What are you doing here, Elijah?"

—1 Kings 19:11b–13

PSALM 71:17–19

O God, from my youth you have taught me,
and I still proclaim your wondrous deeds.
So even to old age and gray hairs,
O God, do not forsake me,
until I proclaim your might
to all the generations to come.

Your power and your righteousness, O God, reach the high heavens.

GOSPEL READING

AT THAT TIME JESUS SAID, "I thank you, Father, Lord of heaven and earth, because you have hidden these things from the wise and the intelligent and have revealed them to infants; yes, Father, for such was your gracious will. All things have been handed over to me by my Father; and no one knows the Son except the Father, and no one knows the Father except the Son and anyone to whom the Son chooses to reveal him.

"Come to me, all you that are weary and are carrying heavy burdens, and I will give you rest. Take my yoke upon you, and learn from me; for I am gentle and humble in heart, and you will find rest for your souls. For my yoke is easy, and my burden is light."

—Matthew 11:25–30

SILENCE

PRAYERS OF THE SAINTS

O true Lord and my Glory! How delicate and extremely heavy a cross You have prepared for those who reach this state! "Delicate" because it is pleasing: "heavy" because there come times when there is no capacity to bear it; and yet the soul would never want to be freed from it unless it were for the sake of being with You. When it recalls that it hasn't served You in anything and that by living it can serve You, it would want to carry a much heavier cross and never die until the end of the world. It finds no rest in anything except in doing You some small service. It doesn't know what it wants, but it well understands that it wants nothing other than You.

—St. Teresa of Avila

PRAYER FOR THE DAY

O God, who has prepared for them that love you unseen good things, pour into our hearts such a sense of your love, that loving you in all, and above all, we may obtain your promises, surpassing all desire. Through Jesus Christ, your Son our Lord, who lives and reigns with you in the unity of the Holy Spirit, God world without end. Amen.

EVENING PRAYER

Tuesday

Theme: Sensitivity of Spirit

FROM THÉRÈSE

What would happen if a clumsy gardener didn't graft his bushes well? What if he didn't know how to recognize the nature of each one, and wanted to make roses bloom on a peach tree? . . . That would kill the tree, which even so was good and was capable of producing fruit.

That is how one must know how to recognize, beginning in childhood, what God asks of souls, and how to second the action of His grace, without ever speeding it up or slowing it down.

PREPARATION

Lord Jesus,
You have much to tell us
if we will attend carefully
to that interior place
where wisdom makes its home.
May we keep well the rooms
of our spiritual house.

GOSPEL SENTENCE

THE PHARISEES AND SADDUCEES CAME, and to test Jesus they asked him to show them a sign from heaven. He answered them, "When it is evening, you say, 'It will be fair weather, for the sky is red.' And in the morning, 'It will be stormy today, for the sky is red and threatening.' You know how to interpret the appearance of the sky, but you cannot interpret the signs of the times. An evil and adulterous generation asks for a sign, but no sign will be given to it except the sign of Jonah." Then he left them and went away.

—Matthew 16:1–4

SILENCE

CONFESSION

Almighty and most merciful God, who drew from a rock a fountain of living water for a thirsting people, draw from the hardness of our hearts tears of contrition, that we may be able to bewail our sins and deserve through your mercy to obtain their remission.

Yet among the mature we do speak wisdom, though it is not a wisdom of this age or of the rulers of this age, who are doomed to perish. But we speak God's wisdom, secret and hidden, which God decreed before the ages for our glory. None of the rulers of this age understood this; for if they had, they would not have crucified the Lord of glory. But, as it is written,

"What no eye has seen, nor ear heard,
nor the human heart conceived,
what God has prepared for those who love him"—

these things God has revealed to us through the Spirit; for the Spirit searches everything, even the depths of God. For what human being knows what is truly human except the human spirit that is within? So also no one comprehends what is truly God's except the Spirit of God. Now we have received not the spirit of the world, but the Spirit that is from God, so that we may understand the gifts bestowed on us by God. And we speak of these things in words not taught by human wisdom but taught by the Spirit, interpreting spiritual things to those who are spiritual.

—1 Corinthians 2:6–13

When I think of your ordinances from of old,
  I take comfort, O LORD.
Hot indignation seizes me because of the
  wicked,
  those who forsake your law.
Your statutes have been my songs
  wherever I make my home.
I remember your name in the night, O LORD,
  and keep your law.
This blessing has fallen to me,
  for I have kept your precepts.

GOSPEL READING

ONCE JESUS WAS ASKED by the Pharisees when the
kingdom of God was coming, and he answered,
"The kingdom of God is not coming with things
that can be observed; nor will they say, 'Look,
here it is!' or 'There it is!' For, in fact, the kingdom of God is among you."

Then he said to the disciples, "The days are
coming when you will long to see one of the days
of the Son of Man, and you will not see it. They
will say to you, 'Look there!' or 'Look here!' Do
not go, do not set off in pursuit. For as the light-
ning flashes and lights up the sky from one side to
the other, so will the Son of Man be in his day.

But first he must endure much suffering and be rejected by this generation."

—Luke 17:20–25

SILENCE

PRAYERS OF THE SAINTS

Blessed Jesus, still my soul in you. Reign in me, O mighty Calm. Rule in me, O gentle King, O peaceful King. Give me self-control, strong self-control over what I say, what I think, what I do. Deliver me, beloved Lord, from fractiousness, irritability, lack of gentleness, and by your own profound patience, give the same to me, with a soul that loves to be still in you. Make me again in your likeness, in this as in everything. Amen. O rest in the Lord forever, my soul, for he is the eternal repose of the saints.

—St. John of the Cross

O God, who made blessed John, thy confessor and doctor, a wonderful lover of self-denial and of the Cross, grant that we, by steadfastly following his example, may attain eternal glory. Through our Lord. Amen.

Protect, O Lord, thy people; and because we have confidence in the intercession of blessed Peter and Paul and thy other apostles, ever defend and preserve us.

May all thy Saints ever help us, we beseech thee, O Lord, and grant that, whilst we honor their merits, we may experience their intercession. Grant thy holy peace unto these our days, and drive all iniquity from thy Church. Direct and prosper unto salvation every step and action and desire of us and of all thy servants. Repay our benefactors with everlasting blessings; and grant eternal rest to all the faithful departed. Through Christ our Lord. Amen.

Wednesday

FROM THÉRÈSE

I'm suffering only for an instant. It's because we think of the past and the future that we become discouraged and fall into despair.

PREPARATION

Lord Jesus,
You understand our temptations
and know our wounds.
Lend to us your strong heart and
peaceful mind, so that these
trials may do their work in us.

GOSPEL SENTENCE

SHE SAID TO HIM, "Declare that these two sons of mine will sit, one at your right had and one at your left, in your kingdom." But Jesus answered, "You do not know what you are asking. Are you able to drink the cup that I am about to drink?"

—Matthew 20:21b–22a

PENITENTIAL PSALM
Psalm 51

Have mercy on me, O God,
   according to your steadfast love;
according to your abundant mercy
   blot out my transgressions.
Wash me thoroughly from my iniquity,
   and cleanse me from my sin.

For I know my transgressions,
   and my sin is ever before me.
Against you, you alone, have I sinned
   and done what is evil in your sight,
so that you are justified in your sentence
   and blameless when you pass judgment.
Indeed, I was born guilty,
   a sinner when my mother conceived me.

You desire truth in the inward being;
   therefore teach me wisdom in my secret heart.
Purge me with hyssop, and I shall be clean;
   wash me, and I shall be whiter than snow.
Let me hear joy and gladness;
   let the ones that you have crushed rejoice.
Hide your face from my sins,
   and blot out all my iniquities.

Create in me a clean heart, O God,
    and put a new and right spirit within me.
Do not cast me away from your presence,
    and do not take your holy spirit from me.
Restore to me the joy of your salvation,
    and sustain in me a willing spirit.

Then I will teach transgressors your ways,
    and sinners will return to you.
Deliver me from bloodshed, O God,
    O God of my salvation,
    and my tongue will sing aloud of your
    deliverance.

O Lord, open my lips,
    and my mouth will declare your praise.
For you have no delight in sacrifice;
    if I were to give a burnt offering, you would
    not be pleased.
The sacrifice acceptable to God is a broken spirit;
    a broken and contrite heart, O God, you will
    not despise.

Do good to Zion in your good pleasure;
    rebuild the walls of Jerusalem,
then you will delight in right sacrifices,
    in burnt offerings and whole burnt offerings;
    then bulls will be offered on your altar.

So we do not lose heart. Even though our outer nature is wasting away, our inner nature is being renewed day by day. For this slight momentary affliction is preparing us for an eternal weight of glory beyond all measure, because we look not at what can be seen but at what cannot be seen; for what can be seen is temporary, but what cannot be seen is eternal.

For we know that if the earthly tent we live in is destroyed, we have a building from God, a house not made with hands, eternal in the heavens. For in this tent we groan, longing to be clothed with our heavenly dwelling—if indeed, when we have taken it off we will not be found naked. For while we are still in this tent, we groan under our burden, because we wish not to be unclothed but to be further clothed, so that what is mortal may be swallowed up by life. He who has prepared us for this very thing is God, who has given us the Spirit as a guarantee.

—2 Corinthians 4:16–5:5

PSALM 119:141–144

I am small and despised,
    yet I do not forget your precepts.
Your righteousness is an everlasting righteousness,
    and your law is the truth.

Trouble and anguish have come upon me,
  but your commandments are my delight.
Your decrees are righteous for ever;
  give me understanding that I may live.

GOSPEL READING

BLESSED ARE THE POOR IN SPIRIT, for theirs is the
  kingdom of heaven.
Blessed are those who mourn, for they will be com-
  forted.
Blessed are the meek, for they will inherit the earth.
Blessed are those who hunger and thirst for right-
  eousness, for they will be filled.
Blessed are the merciful, for they will receive mercy.
Blessed are the pure in heart, for they will see God.
Blessed are the peacemakers, for they will be called
  children of God.
Blessed are those who are persecuted for righteous-
  ness' sake, for theirs is the kingdom of heaven.

Blessed are you when people revile you and per-
secute you and utter all kinds of evil against you
falsely on my account. Rejoice and be glad, for
your reward is great in heaven, for in the same
way they persecuted the prophets who were
before you.

—Matthew 5:3–12

SILENCE

PRAYERS OF THE SAINTS

O almighty God, seeing that amid so many grievous troubles, by reason of our weakness, we continually fall away, grant that through the merits and mediation of your only Son in his blessed passion, we may be mercifully relieved. Who lives and reigns with you in the unity of the Holy Spirit, God world without end. Amen.

PRAYER FOR THE DAY

Mercifully consider our weakness, O almighty God, and whereas the strain of our own actions bears us down may the intercession of thy blessed and glorious martyrs be our shield of strength. Through Jesus Christ, thy Son our Lord, who liveth and reigneth with thee in the unity of the Holy Ghost, God world without end. Amen.

Wednesday

FROM THÉRÈSE

God forgive me, but He knows that I try to practice my faith, even though it brings me no joy. I have made more acts of faith in the last year than during all the rest of my life.

Whenever I find myself faced with the prospect of an attack by the enemy, I am most courageous; I turn my back on him, without so much as looking at him, and run to Jesus. I tell Him I am ready to shed all my blood to prove my faith in heaven.

PREPARATION

God in Heaven,
Prepare us to do the hard things.
Remind us of your purpose,
which streams through
all that we do and hovers over
all that happens to us.
Hold our frail selves next to your heart
to help our will, our endurance, our faith.

GOSPEL SENTENCE

BROTHER WILL BETRAY BROTHER to death, and a father his child, and children will rise against parents and have them put to death; and you will be hated by all because of my name. But the one who endures to the end will be saved.

—Matthew 10:21–22

SILENCE

CONFESSION

O God, who shows the light of your truth to those who are astray, that they may return to the way of righteousness, grant that all who belong to the Christian faith may shun what is not, and follow what is, in accordance with this Name. Through Jesus Christ, your Son our Lord, who lives and reigns with you in the unity of the Holy Spirit, God world without end. Amen.

FIRST READING

And I heard a loud voice from the throne saying,
"See, the home of God is among mortals.
He will dwell with them;
they will be his peoples,

and God himself will be with them;
he will wipe every tear from their eyes.
Death will be no more;
mourning and crying and pain will be no more,
for the first things have passed away."

—Revelation 21:3–4

PSALM 139:7–12

Where can I go from your spirit?
Or where can I flee from your presence?
If I ascend to heaven, you are there;
if I make my bed in Sheol, you are there.
If I take the wings of the morning
and settle at the farthest limits of the sea,
even there your hand shall lead me,
and your right hand shall hold me fast.
If I say, "Surely the darkness shall cover me,
and the light around me become night,"
even the darkness is not dark to you;
the night is as bright as the day,
for darkness is as light to you.

GOSPEL READING

"YOU ARE THE ONES who have stood by me in my
trials; and I confer on you, just as my Father has
conferred on me, a kingdom, so that you may eat
and drink at my table in my kingdom, and you

will sit on thrones judging the twelve tribes of Israel.

"Simon, Simon, listen! Satan has demanded to sift all of you like wheat, but I have prayed for you that your own faith may not fail; and you, when once you have turned back, strengthen your brothers." And he said to him, "Lord, I am ready to go with you to prison and to death!" Jesus said, "I tell you, Peter, the cock will not crow this day, until you have denied three times that you know me."

—Luke 22:28–34

SILENCE

PRAYERS OF THE SAINTS

My God, here I am all devoted to Thee: Lord, make me according to Thy heart.

—Brother Lawrence of the Resurrection

PRAYER FOR NIGHTTIME

O God, who in thy wonderful providence hast been pleased to appoint thy holy angels for our guardians: mercifully hear our prayers, and grant we may rest secure under their protection, and enjoy their fellowship in heaven for ever. Through Christ our Lord. Amen.

MORNING PRAYER
Thursday
Theme: Trust in God's Grace

FROM THÉRÈSE

How happy God makes me! It is so pleasant and easy to serve Him during this life. Yes, I shall always go on saying that He has given me what I wanted, or rather, that He has made me want what He wished to give me.

PREPARATION

May we cling, O Lord,
to your great promises to us.
May we expect wondrous works
from your hands
and be pleased—but never surprised—
by the miracles you visit upon us
day after day.

GOSPEL SENTENCE

HE WENT UP THE MOUNTAIN and called to him those whom he wanted, and they came to him. And he appointed twelve, whom he also named apostles, to be with him, and to be sent out to proclaim the message, and to have authority to cast out demons.

—Mark 3:13–15

SILENCE

PENITENTIAL PSALM
Psalm 102

Hear my prayer, O LORD;
  let my cry come to you.
Do not hide your face from me
  in the day of my distress.
Incline your ear to me;
  answer me speedily in the day when I call.

For my days pass away like smoke,
  and my bones burn like a furnace.
My heart is stricken and withered like grass;
  I am too wasted to eat my bread.
Because of my loud groaning
  my bones cling to my skin.
I am like an owl of the wilderness,
  like a little owl of the waste places.
I lie awake;
  I am like a lonely bird on the housetop.

All day long my enemies taunt me;
  those who deride me use my name for a curse.
For I eat ashes like bread,
  and mingle tears with my drink,
because of your indignation and anger;
  for you have lifted me up and thrown me aside.
My days are like an evening shadow;
  I wither away like grass.

But you, O LORD, are enthroned for ever;
  your name endures to all generations.
You will rise up and have compassion on Zion,
  for it is time to favor it;
  the appointed time has come.
For your servants hold its stones dear,
  and have pity on its dust.
The nations will fear the name of the LORD,
  and all the kings of the earth your glory.
For the LORD will build up Zion;
  he will appear in his glory.
He will regard the prayer of the destitute,
  and will not despise their prayer.

Let this be recorded for a generation to come,
  so that a people yet unborn may praise the
  LORD:
that he looked down from his holy height,
  from heaven the LORD looked at the earth,
to hear the groans of the prisoners,
  to set free those who were doomed to die;

so that the name of the LORD may be declared
   in Zion,
      and his praise in Jerusalem,
when peoples gather together,
   and kingdoms, to worship the LORD.

He has broken my strength in midcourse;
   he has shortened my days.
"O my God," I say, "do not take me away
   at the midpoint of my life,
you whose years endure
   throughout all generations."

Long ago you laid the foundation of the earth,
   and the heavens are the work of your hands.
They will perish, but you endure;
   they will all wear out like a garment.
You change them like clothing, and they pass
   away;
      but you are the same, and your years have no
      end.
The children of your servants shall live secure;
   their offspring shall be established in your
   presence.

FIRST READING

I said, "Woe is me! I am lost, for I am a man of
unclean lips, and I live among a people of unclean

lips; yet my eyes have seen the King, the LORD of hosts!"

Then one of the seraphs flew to me, holding a live coal that had been taken from the altar with a pair of tongs. The seraph touched my mouth with it and said: "Now that this has touched your lips, your guilt has departed and your sin is blotted out." Then I heard the voice of the Lord saying, "Whom shall I send, and who will go for us?" And I said, "Here am I; send me!"

—Isaiah 6:5–8

PSALM 89:1–4

I will sing of your steadfast love, O LORD, forever;
    with my mouth I will proclaim your faithful-
    ness to all generations.
I declare that your steadfast love is established
    for ever;
    your faithfulness is as firm as the heavens.
You said, "I have made a covenant with my chosen
    one,
    I have sworn to my servant David:
'I will establish your descendants for ever,
    and build your throne for all generations.'"

AND MARY SAID,

"My soul magnifies the Lord,
  and my spirit rejoices in God my Savior,
for he has looked with favor on the lowliness of
  his servant.
  Surely, from now on all generations will call
  me blessed;
for the Mighty One has done great things for
  me,
and holy is his name.
His mercy is for those who fear him
  from generation to generation.
He has shown strength with his arm;
  he has scattered the proud in the thoughts of
  their hearts.
He has brought down the powerful from their
  thrones,
  and lifted up the lowly;
he has filled the hungry with good things,
  and sent the rich away empty.
He has helped his servant Israel,
  in remembrance of his mercy,
according to the promise he made to our ancestors,
  to Abraham and to his descendants forever."

—Luke 1:46–55

SILENCE

PRAYERS OF THE SAINTS

O God, who has honored the Order of Carmel with the special title of thy blessed Mother Mary, ever virgin, grant, in thy mercy, that we, who keep her memory, may be shielded by her protection and be found worthy to attain joy everlasting. Amen.

PRAYER FOR THE DAY

O God, our refuge and strength, the very author of all goodness, hear the devout prayers of your Church; and grant that what we confidently ask, we may effectually obtain. Through Jesus Christ, your Son our Lord, who lives and reigns with you in the unity of the Holy Spirit, God world without end. Amen.

EVENING PRAYER

Thursday

Theme: Trust in God's Care

FROM THÉRÈSE

If you find me dead one morning, don't be grieved. . . . Without a doubt it's a great grace to receive the sacraments; but when God doesn't permit it, it's good just the same; everything is grace.

PREPARATION

Lord Jesus, you have blessed us
and keep blessing us with all your riches,
with heavenly favor, with strength and wisdom,
with the privileges of those who are children
of the Most High.
Give us the ability to hold within us
the truth of all this grace, and to depend upon it.
May we rely each day on your faithfulness.

GOSPEL SENTENCE

JESUS . . . ORDERED THE MAN to be brought to him; and when he came near, he asked him,

"What do you want me to do for you?" He said, "Lord, let me see again." Jesus said to him, "Receive your sight; your faith has saved you." Immediately he regained his sight and followed him, glorifying God; and all the people, when they saw it, praised God.

—Luke 18:40–43

SILENCE

CONFESSION

Almighty, everlasting God, who in the abundance of your loving kindness exceeds both the merits and prayers of those who call on you, pour down upon us your mercy, that you may forgive what our conscience fears and grant what we venture not to ask. Through Jesus Christ your Son our Lord, who lives and reigns with you in the unity of the Holy Spirit, God world without end Amen.

FIRST READING

Blessed be the God and Father of our Lord Jesus Christ, who has blessed us in Christ with every spiritual blessing in the heavenly places, just as he chose us in Christ before the foundation of the world to be holy and blameless before him in love. He destined us for adoption as his children through Jesus Christ, according to the good pleasure of his will, to the praise of his glorious grace that he freely bestowed on us in the Beloved. In him we have redemption through his blood, the forgiveness of our trespasses, according to the riches of his grace that he lavished upon us. With all wisdom and insight he has made known to us the mystery of his will, according to his good pleasure that he set forth in Christ, as a plan for the fullness of time, to gather up all things in him, things in heaven and things on earth.

—Ephesians 1:3–10

PSALM 70:4–5

Let all who seek you
rejoice and be glad in you.
Let those who love your salvation
say evermore, "God is great!"
But I am poor and needy;
hasten to me, O God!
You are my help and my deliverer;
O Lord, do not delay!

GOSPEL READING

"Do not let your hearts be troubled. Believe in God, believe also in me. In my Father's house there are many dwelling places. If it were not so, would I have told you that I go to prepare a place for you? And if I go and prepare a place for you, I will come again and will take you to myself, so that where I am, there you may be also. And you know the way to the place where I am going." Thomas said to him, "Lord, we do not know where you are going. How can we know the way?" Jesus said to him, "I am the way, and the truth, and the life. No one comes to the Father except through me. If you know me, you will know my Father also. From now on you do know him and have seen him."

—John 14:1–7

SILENCE

PRAYERS OF THE SAINTS

God our Father,
  source of all holiness,
  the work of your hands is manifest in your
  saints,
  the beauty of your truth is reflected in their
  faith.

May we who aspire to have part in their joy
    be filled with the Spirit that blessed their lives,
    so that having shared their faith on earth
    we may also know their peace in your kingdom.
Grant this through Christ our Lord. Amen.

PRAYER FOR NIGHTTIME

Visit, we beseech thee, O Lord, this house and family, and drive far from it all snares of the enemy: let thy holy angels dwell herein, who may keep us in peace, and may thy blessing be always upon us. Through Jesus Christ our Lord, thy Son, who liveth and reigneth with thee, in the unity of the Holy Ghost, God world without end. Amen.

MORNING PRAYER

Friday

Theme: Humility in All Things

FROM THÉRÈSE

If all the weak and imperfect souls felt what the smallest of all souls feels, the soul of your little Thérèse, not a single one would despair of arriving at the top of the mountain of love, since Jesus does not ask for great actions, but only for abandonment and gratefulness.

PREPARATION

Lord God,
Help us remember that all we have
comes from you—our abilities,
our gifts, our riches, our opportunities.
May we receive them in gratitude
and rejoice also for your generosity to all.

GOSPEL SENTENCE

AT THAT SAME HOUR Jesus rejoiced in the Holy Spirit and said, "I thank you, Father, Lord of heaven and earth, because you have hidden these things from the wise and the intelligent and have revealed them to infants; yes, Father, for such was your gracious will."

—Luke 10:21

SILENCE

PENITENTIAL PSALM
Psalm 130

Out of the depths I cry to you, O LORD.
Lord, hear my voice!
Let your ears be attentive
to the voice of my supplications!

If you, O LORD, should mark iniquities,
Lord, who could stand?
But there is forgiveness with you,
so that you may be revered.

I wait for the LORD, my soul waits,
and in his word I hope;
my soul waits for the Lord
more than those who watch for the morning,
more than those who watch for the morning.

O Israel, hope in the LORD!
For with the LORD there is steadfast love,
and with him is great power to redeem.

It is he who will redeem Israel
   from all its iniquities.

FIRST READING

Seek the LORD while he may be found,
   call upon him while he is near;
let the wicked forsake their way,
   and the unrighteous their thoughts;
let them return to the LORD, that he may have
   mercy on them,
   and to our God, for he will abundantly pardon.
For my thoughts are not your thoughts,
   nor are your ways my ways, says the LORD.
For as the heavens are higher than the earth,
   so are my ways higher than your ways
   and my thoughts than your thoughts.
                                        —Isaiah 55:6–9

PSALM 103:11–14

For as the heavens are high above the earth,
   so great is his steadfast love toward those who
   fear him;
as far as the east is from the west,
   so far he removes our transgressions from us.
As a father has compassion for his children,
   so the LORD has compassion for those who
   fear him.

For he knows how we were made;
    he remembers that we are dust.

GOSPEL READING

FOR THE KINGDOM OF HEAVEN is like a landowner who went out early in the morning to hire laborers for his vineyard. After agreeing with the laborers for the usual daily wage, he sent them into his vineyard. . . . And about five o'clock he went out and found others standing around; and he said to them, "Why are you standing here idle all day?" They said to him, "Because no one has hired us." He said to them, "You also go into the vineyard." When evening came, the owner of the vineyard said to his manager, "Call the laborers and give them their pay, beginning with the last and then going to the first." When those hired about five o'clock came, each of them received the usual daily wage. Now when the first came, they thought they would receive more; but each of them also received the usual daily wage. And when they received it, they grumbled against the landowner, saying, "These last worked only one hour, and you have made them equal to us who have borne the burden of the day and the scorching heat." But he replied to one of them, "Friend, I am doing you no wrong; did you not agree with me for the usual daily wage? Take what belongs to you and go; I choose to give to this last the same as I give to you. Am I not allowed to do what I choose with what belongs to me? Or are you envious because I am generous?" So the last will be first, and the first will be last.

—Matthew 20:1–2, 6–16

SILENCE

PRAYERS OF THE SAINTS

O Brightness of the Father's glory! bringing light from the light! Thou light of light, and fount of light, and day that illuminest the day!

O thou true sun! Pour forth thy rays on us, shining upon us with unfading splendor! O radiance of the Holy Ghost, be thou infused into our senses and powers.

Give us, also, to invoke the Father, the Father of eternal glory, the Father of mighty grace, that he would drive from us sin and its allurements.

May he give energy to our deeds and strengthen them; may he break the teeth of the envious serpent; may he support us when we rudely fall, and give us the grace to act.

May he govern and rule our mind, in a chaste and faithful body; may our faith be fervent in warmth, void of the poisons of error.

May Christ be our food, and faith our drink; may we in gladness quaff the sober inebriation of the Spirit.

May this day be one of joy; modesty its dawn, faith its noon; and no night to dim the mind.

The aurora is swiftly advancing; O may the full Aurora come, the whole Son in the Father, and the whole Father in his Word!

To God the Father, and to his only Son, and to the Paraclete Spirit, be glory for ever and ever. Amen.

—Hymn of St. Ambrose

PRAYER FOR THE DAY

You know my weakness, Lord. Every morning I make a resolution to practice humility and in the evening I recognize that I have committed again many faults of pride. At this I am tempted to become discouraged but I know that discouragement is also pride.

Therefore, O my God, I want to base my hope in you alone. Since you can do everything, deign to bring to birth in my soul the virtue I desire. To obtain this grace of your infinite mercy I will very often repeat: "O Jesus, gentle and humble of heart, make my heart like yours!"

—St. Thérèse of Lisieux

EVENING PRAYER

Friday

Theme: Humility in All Things

FROM THÉRÈSE

Even if I had accomplished all the works of St. Paul, I would still believe myself to be a "useless servant." But it is precisely this that makes up my joy, for having nothing, I shall receive everything from God.

PREPARATION

Dear Jesus,
We rely on you for everything,
but sometimes we forget that.
Help us forget our deeds and efforts
and remember your kindness.
Help us forget our virtues
and remember your grace toward us.

GOSPEL SENTENCE

NO ONE CAN COME TO ME unless drawn by the Father who sent me; and I will raise that person up on the last day. It is written in the prophets, "And they shall all be taught by God."

—John 6:44–45a

SILENCE

CONFESSION

O almighty and most merciful God, who didst draw from a rock a fountain of living water for a thirsting people, draw from the hardness of our hearts tears of contrition, that we may be able to bewail our sins and deserve through thy mercy to obtain their remission.

FIRST READING

Everyone is stupid and without knowledge;
   goldsmiths are all put to shame by their idols;
for their images are false,
   and there is no breath in them.
They are worthless, a work of delusion;
   at the time of their punishment they shall perish.
Not like these is the LORD, the portion of Jacob,
   for he is the one who formed all things,
and Israel is the tribe of his inheritance;
   the LORD of hosts is his name. . . .

I know, O LORD, that the way of human beings
   is not in their control,
that mortals as they walk cannot direct their steps.
Correct me, O LORD, but in just measure;
not in your anger, or you will bring me to
   nothing.

                        —Jeremiah 10:14–16, 23–24

PSALM 76:7–12

You indeed are awesome!
   Who can stand before you when once your
   anger is roused?
From the heavens you uttered judgment;
   the earth feared and was still
when God rose up to establish judgment,
   to save all the oppressed of the earth.

Human wrath serves only to praise you,
   when you bind the last bit of your wrath
   around you.
Make vows to the LORD your God, and perform
   them;
   let all who are around him bring gifts to the
   one who is awesome,
who cuts off the spirit of princes,
   who inspires fear in the kings of the earth.

AFTER THIS HE WENT OUT and saw a tax collector named Levi, sitting at the tax booth; and he said to him, "Follow me." And he got up, left everything, and followed him.

Then Levi gave a great banquet for him in his house; and there was a large crowd of tax-collectors and others sitting at the table with them. The Pharisees and their scribes were complaining to his disciples, saying, "Why do you eat and drink with tax collectors and sinners?" Jesus answered, "Those who are well have no need of a physician, but those who are sick; I have come to call not the righteous but sinners to repentance."

—Luke 5:27–32

SILENCE

PRAYERS OF THE SAINTS

May you be blessed for ever! Although I abandoned You, You did not abandon me so completely as not to turn to raise me up by always holding out Your hand to me. And oftentimes, Lord, I did not want it; nor did I desire to understand how often You called me again.

—St. Teresa of Avila

Graciously hear us, O God our Savior; that as we rejoice in the life of Teresa, so we may be nourished with the food of her heavenly doctrine, and be enlightened by the affection of loving devotion. Through Christ our Lord. Amen.

PRAYER FOR NIGHTTIME

God our Father, you have promised your kingdom to those who are willing to become like little children. Help us to follow the way of St. Thérèse with confidence so that by her prayers we may come to know your eternal glory.

—Opening prayer for her feast day Mass

MORNING PRAYER
Saturday

Theme: Living by the Little Way

FROM THÉRÈSE

So you see, Mother, what a very little soul I am! I can only offer very little things to God. These little sacrifices bring great peace of soul, but I often let the chance of making them slip by. However, it does not discourage me. I put up with having a little less peace, and try to be more careful the next time.

PREPARATION

Lord Jesus, restore to us
the heart of a child, open and ever hopeful,
trusting completely in you
and therefore afraid of nothing else.

GOSPEL SENTENCE

JESUS SAID, "Let the little children come to me, and do not stop them; for it is to such as these that the kingdom of heaven belongs."

—Matthew 19:14

PENITENTIAL PSALM
Psalm 143

Hear my prayer, O LORD;
give ear to my supplications in your faithfulness;
answer me in your righteousness.
Do not enter into judgment with your servant,
for no one living is righteous before you.

For the enemy has pursued me,
crushing my life to the ground,
making me sit in darkness like those long dead.
Therefore my spirit faints within me;
my heart within me is appalled.

I remember the days of old,
I think about all your deeds,
I meditate on the works of your hands.
I stretch out my hands to you;
my soul thirsts for you like a parched land.

Answer me quickly, O LORD;
my spirit fails.
Do not hide your face from me,
or I shall be like those who go down to the Pit.
Let me hear of your steadfast love in the morning,
for in you I put my trust.

Teach me the way I should go,
for to you I lift up my soul.

Save me, O LORD, from my enemies;
I have fled to you for refuge.
Teach me to do your will,
for you are my God.
Let your good spirit lead me
on a level path.

For your name's sake, O LORD,
preserve my life.
In your righteousness bring me out
of trouble.
In your steadfast love cut off my enemies,
and destroy all my adversaries,
for I am your servant.

FIRST READING

Indeed, the body does not consist of one member
but of many. If the foot would say, "Because I am
not a hand, I do not belong to the body," that
would not make it any less a part of the body. . . .
If the whole body were an eye, where would the
hearing be? If the whole body were hearing,
where would the sense of smell be? But as it is,
God arranged the members in the body, each one
of them, as he chose. . . . The eye cannot say to

the hand, "I have no need of you," nor again the head to the feet, "I have no need of you." On the contrary, the members of the body that seem to be weaker are indispensable, and those members of the body that we think less honorable we clothe with greater honor. . . . But God has so arranged the body, giving the greater honor to the inferior member, that there may be no dissension within the body, but the members may have the same care for one another. If one member suffers, all suffer together with it; if one member is honored, all rejoice together with it.

—1 Corinthians 12:14–15, 17–18,
21–23a, 24b–26

PSALM 27:1, 4

The LORD is my light and my salvation;
  whom shall I fear?
The LORD is the stronghold of my life;
  of whom shall I be afraid?
. . .
One thing I asked of the LORD,
  that will I seek after:
to live in the house of the LORD
  all the days of my life,
to behold the beauty of the LORD,
  and to inquire in his temple.

THEN THE KING WILL SAY to those at his right hand, "Come, you that are blessed by my Father, inherit the kingdom prepared for you from the foundation of the world; for I was hungry and you gave me food, I was thirsty and you gave me something to drink, I was a stranger and you welcomed me, I was naked and you gave me clothing, I was sick and you took care of me, I was in prison and you visited me." Then the righteous will answer him, "Lord, when was it that we saw you hungry and gave you food, or thirsty and gave you something to drink? And when was it that we saw you a stranger and welcomed you, or naked and gave you clothing? And when was it that we saw you sick or in prison and visited you?" And the king will answer them, "Truly I tell you, just as you did it to one of the least of these who are members of my family, you did it to me."

—Matthew 25:34–40

SILENCE

O eternal God,
Turn us into the arms and hands,
the legs and feet
of your beloved Son, Jesus.
You gave birth to him in heaven
before the creation of the earth.
You gave birth to us on earth,
to become his living body.
Make us worthy to be his limbs,
and so worthy to share
in his eternal bliss.

—Hildegard of Bingen

PRAYER FOR THE DAY

My God, I offer you all that I do today for the intentions and the glory of the Sacred Heart of Jesus. I want to sanctify every beat of my heart, my thoughts and my simplest works by uniting them to his infinite merits. I want to repair for my faults by casting them into the furnace of his merciful love.

O my God! I ask you for myself and those dear to me the grace to fulfill perfectly your holy will and to accept for love of you the joys and sorrows of this passing life so that one day we may be reunited in heaven for all eternity. Amen.

—St. Thérèse of Lisieux

EVENING PRAYER
Saturday

Theme: Living by the Little Way

FROM THÉRÈSE

It's not Martha's works that Jesus blamed. Those works are the ones His divine Mother humbly accepted to do her whole life, since she had to prepare the meals for the Holy Family. It's only the anxiousness of his eager hostess that he wanted to amend.

PREPARATION

Lord, we show our love for you
day by day, in simple small ways.
Help us find holy purpose in every task
and the means to demonstrate your care
for others in every interaction.

GOSPEL SENTENCE

THE LORD REPLIED, "If you had faith the size of a mustard seed, you could say to this mulberry tree, 'Be uprooted and planted in the sea,' and it would obey you."

—Luke 17:6

CONFESSION

O Jesus! how happy I would be if I had been faithful, but alas! often in the evening I am sad because I feel I could have corresponded better with your graces. . . . And yet, O my God, very far from becoming discouraged at the sight of my miseries, I come to you with confidence, recalling that "those who are well do not need a doctor but the sick do." I beg you, then, to cure me and to pardon me. . . . I beg you, O my Divine Bridegroom, to be the Restorer of my soul, to act in me despite my resistance; and lastly, I wish to have no other will but yours. Tomorrow, with the help of your grace, I will begin a new life in which each moment will be an act of love.

—St. Thérèse of Lisieux

FIRST READING

If I speak in the tongues of mortals and of angels, but do not have love, I am a noisy gong or a clanging cymbal. And if I have prophetic powers, and understand all mysteries and all knowledge, and if I have all faith, so as to remove mountains, but do not have love, I am nothing. If I give away all my possessions, and if I hand over my body so that I

may boast, but do not have love, I gain nothing. . . .
Love never ends. But as for prophecies, they will
come to an end; as for tongues, they will cease; as
for knowledge, it will come to an end. For we know
only in part and we prophesy only in part, but
when the complete comes, the partial will come to
an end. . . . And now faith, hope, and love abide,
these three; and the greatest of these is love.
                    —1 Corinthians 13:1–3, 8–10, 13

PSALM 90:1–2, 9–10, 14–17

Lord, you have been our dwelling place
    in all generations.
Before the mountains were brought forth,
    or ever you had formed the earth and the
    world,
    from everlasting to everlasting you are God.
. . .
For all our days pass away under your wrath;
    our years come to an end like a sigh.
The days of our life are seventy years,
    or perhaps eighty, if we are strong;
even then their span is only toil and trouble;
    they are soon gone, and we fly away.
. . .
Satisfy us in the morning with your steadfast love,
    so that we may rejoice and be glad all our days.

Make us glad as many days as you have afflicted us,
    and as many years as we have seen evil.
Let your work be manifest to your servants,
    and your glorious power to their children.
Let the favor of the Lord our God be upon us,
    and prosper for us the work of our hands—
    O prosper the work of our hands!

GOSPEL READING

NOW AS THEY WENT ON THEIR WAY, he entered a certain village, where a woman named Martha welcomed him into her home. She had a sister named Mary, who sat at the Lord's feet and listened to what he was saying. But Martha was distracted by her many tasks; so she came to him and asked, "Lord, do you not care that my sister has left me to do all the work by myself? Tell her then to help me." But the Lord answered her, "Martha, Martha, you are worried and distracted by many things; there is need of only one thing. Mary has chosen the better part, which will not be taken away from her."

—Luke 10:38–42

SILENCE

God be in my head,
 And in my understanding;
God be in my eyes,
 And in my looking;
God be in my mouth
 And in my speaking;
God be in my heart,
 And in my thinking;
God be at my end and at my departing.

       —Sarum Primer

PRAYER FOR NIGHTTIME

O God, Creator of all things, and ruler of the heavens, 'tis Thou that clothest day with beautiful light, and night with the grace of sleep.

Tis sleep that restores our wearied limbs to the toil of work. Sleep gives repose to the mind when tired, and takes away anxious grief.

The day is spent, and the night is come; we offer thee our thanks and prayers, singing our hymn, that thou mayst help us, thy servants.

May our inmost heart sing thy praise, and tuneful voices sound forth thy name; may our chaste affection love, and our sober mind adore thee.

And when the night's deep gloom shall shut out the day, may our faith know nought of darkness, and the very night be day by faith.

Let not our soul, but only sin feel sleep; let faith keep us chaste, and, by its refreshing power, check the vapors of sleep.

May our heart's deepest self, unshackled by the allurements of sense, dream of thee; nor let the fear of the enemy, whose envy is ever laying snares, disturb us when at rest.

Let our prayer ascend to Christ and to the Father, and to the spirit of Christ and of the Father; O Trinity, one in essence and all powerful, be merciful to us, who pray to thee. Amen.

—Hymn of St. Ambrose

IV
PRAYERS AND POEMS of
St. Thérèse

THÉRÈSE NEVER WROTE A BOOK OF PRAYERS, and most of the prayers she did compose simply happened in the course of her other writing—the story of her soul's development, which she wrote at the request of superiors, and in her numerous letters.

A few prayers, however, were more specific and intentional. We can almost see the words flowing out of her many hours of prayer, as she tried to put into words her deepest desires and spiritual goals so that she could better pursue them. Once on paper, these intentions could be folded and kept as secrets of the heart, or they could be read again and again, kept in the front of her vision. In a few cases, it appears that she shared these prayers with others, for their own spiritual encouragement.

{OO}

AN ACT OF OBLATION AS A VICTIM OF DIVINE LOVE

This prayer marks a turning point in Thérèse's life; privately during a Mass on June 9, 1895, she offered herself as a sacrifice to God's love. She considered this prayer event significant enough to include in a list of her "days of grace," which began with her birth and baptism, included her conversion and audience with the Pope, and continued with the several stages of her formation as a Carmelite nun. After "Taking of the Veil"—meaning her final vows—is listed "Act of Oblation." She invited her sister Céline and others to make a similar profession. This prayer, written in her own hand, was tucked into her copy of the Gospels, which she is said to have carried with her day and night.

Language has been slightly adapted for readability.

O my God, O Most Blessed Trinity, I desire to love You and to make You loved—to labor for the glory of Holy Church by saving souls here upon earth and by delivering those suffering in Purgatory. I desire to fulfill perfectly Your Holy Will, and to reach the degree of glory You have prepared for me in Your Kingdom. In a word, I wish to be holy, but, knowing how helpless I am, I ask You, my God, to be Yourself my holiness.

Since You have loved me so much as to give me Your Only-Begotten Son to be my Savior and my Spouse, the infinite treasures of His merits are mine. Gladly do I offer them to You, and I beg You to behold me only through the eyes of Jesus, and in His Heart aflame with love. Moreover, I offer You all the merits of the Saints both of Heaven and of earth, together with their acts of love, and those of the holy Angels. Lastly, I offer You, O Blessed Trinity, the love and the merits of the Blessed Virgin, my dearest Mother—to her I commit this

Oblation, asking her to present it to You.

During the days of His life on earth her Divine son, my sweet Spouse, spoke these words: "If you ask the Father anything in My Name, He will give it you." Therefore I am certain You will fulfill my longing. O my God, I know that the more You wish to bestow, the more You make us desire. In my heart I feel boundless desires, and I confidently ask You to take possession of my soul. I cannot receive You in Holy Communion as often as I should wish;* but, O Lord, are You not all-powerful? Abide in me as You do in the Tabernacle—never abandon Your Little Victim. I long to console You for ungrateful sinners, and I implore You to take from me all liberty to sin. If through weakness I should chance to fall, may a glance from Your Eyes straightway cleanse my soul, and consume all my imperfections—as fire transforms all things into itself.

I thank You, O my God, for all the graces You have granted me: especially for having purified me in the crucible of suffering. At the Day of Judgment I shall gaze on You with joy, as You bear Your scepter of the Cross. And since You have given me this precious Cross as my portion, I hope to be like You in Paradise and to behold the Sacred Wounds of Your Passion shine on my glorified body.

* In Thérèse's day, it was unusual for Christians—even nuns—to partake of the Eucharist on a frequent basis—perhaps once every few weeks, or certainly not more than once a week.

After earth's exile I trust to possess You in the Home of our Father; but I do not seek to lay up treasures in Heaven. I wish to labor for Your Love alone—with the sole aim of pleasing You, of consoling Your Sacred Heart, and of saving souls who will love You through eternity.

When comes the evening of life, I shall stand before You with empty hands, because I do not ask You, my God, to take account of my works. All our works of justice are blemished in Your eyes. I wish therefore to be robed with Your own Justice, and to receive from Your Love the everlasting gift of Yourself. I desire no other Throne, no other Crown but You, O my Beloved!

In Your sight time is nothing—"one day is a thousand years." You can in a single instant prepare me to appear before You.

In order that my life may be one Act of perfect Love, I offer myself as a Victim of Holocaust to Your Merciful Love, imploring You to consume me unceasingly, and to allow the floods of infinite tenderness gathered up in You to overflow into my soul, that so I may become an absolute martyr of Your Love, O my God! May this martyrdom, after having prepared me to appear in Your Presence, free me from this life at the last, and may my soul take its flight—without delay—into the eternal embrace of Your Merciful love!

O my Beloved, I desire at every beat of my heart to renew this Oblation an infinite number of times, "till the shadows retire," and everlastingly I can tell You my love face to face.

MARY FRANCES TERESA OF THE CHILD
JESUS AND OF THE HOLY FACE.

The ninth of June, Feast of the Most Blessed Trinity, in the year of grace, 1895.

∞

A PRAYER TO OBTAIN HUMILITY

O Jesus! When you were a wayfarer upon earth, you said, "Learn of me, for I am meek and humble of heart, and you shall find rest for your souls." O Almighty King of Heaven! my soul indeed finds rest in seeing you condescend to wash the feet of your apostles, "having taken the form of a slave." I recall the words you uttered to teach me the practice of humility: "I have given you an example, that as I have done to you, so you do also. The servant is not greater than his Lord. . . . If you know these things, you shall be blessed if you do them." I understand, dear Lord, these words which come from your meek and humble heart, and I wish to put them in practice with the help of your grace.

I desire to be humble myself in all sincerity, and to submit my will to that of my sisters, without ever contradicting them, and without questioning whether they have the right to command. No one, O my Beloved! had that right over you, and yet you obeyed not only the Blessed Virgin and St. Joseph, but even your executioners. And now, in the Holy Eucharist, I see you complete your self-abasement. O Divine King of Glory, with wondrous humility, you submitted yourself to all your priests, without any distinction between those who love you and those who, alas! are lukewarm or cold in your service. They may advance or delay the hour of the Holy Sacrifice: you are always ready to come down from Heaven at their call.

O my Beloved, under the white Eucharistic Veil you indeed appear to me meek and humble of heart! To teach me humility, you cannot further abase yourself, and so I wish to respond to your love by putting myself in the lowest place, by sharing your humiliations, so that I may "have a part with you" in the Kingdom of Heaven.

I implore you, dear Jesus, to send me a humiliation whenever I try to set myself above others.

And yet, dear Lord, you know my weakness. Each morning I resolve to be humble, and in the evening I recognize that I have often been guilty of pride. The sight of these faults tempts me to discouragement; yet I know that discouragement is itself but a form of pride. I wish, therefore, O my God, to build all my trust upon you. As you can do all things, plant in my soul this virtue which I desire, and to obtain it from your infinite mercy, I will often say to you: "Jesus, meek and humble of heart, make my heart like yours."

✦

O Jesus, the tender way You lead my soul is beyond all telling. From Easter, the radiant feast of Your triumph, until May, a storm was raging in its depths, but then the dark night was lit by the pure rays of the light of Your grace.

✦

Jesus, my Love,
I have at last found my vocation; it is love! I have found my place in the Church's heart, the place You Yourself have given me, my God. Yes, there in the heart of Mother Church I will be love; so shall I be all things, so shall my dreams come true.

✦

Thérèse was not known as a poet in an artistic sense; yet she wrote numerous poems to accompany life in the convent. She composed verses for special occasions among the sisters there. She also wrote verses that, for all practical purposes, were personal prayers and spiritual reflections. In this

sense, there is little distinction between her written prayers and her poems; both expressed her
spirituality with passion and directness.

✺

MY SONG OF TODAY

1.

Oh! how I love Thee, Jesus! my soul aspires to
   Thee—
and yet for one day only my simple prayer I pray!
Come reign within my heart, smile tenderly on
   me,
        Today, dear Lord, today.

2.

But if I dare take thought of what the morrow
   brings—
That fills my fickle heart with dreary, dull dismay;
I crave, indeed, my God, trials and sufferings,
        But only for today!

3.

O sweetest Star of heaven! O Virgin, spotless,
   blest,
Shining with Jesus' light, guiding to Him my way!
O Mother! 'neath thy veil let my tired spirit rest,
        For this brief passing day!

4.
Soon shall I fly afar among the holy choirs,
Then shall be mine the joy that never knows
    decay;
And then my lips shall sing, to heaven's angelic
    lyres,
            The eternal, glad Today!

                                    June 1894

TO THE SACRED HEART

Beside the tomb wept Magdalen at dawn—
    She sought to find the dead and buried Christ;
Nothing could fill the void now He was gone,
    No one to soothe her burning grief sufficed.
Not even you, Archangels heaven-assigned!
    To her could bring content that dreary day.
Your buried King, alone, she longed to find,
    And bear His lifeless body far away.

Beside His tomb she there the last remained,
    And there again was she before the sun;
There, too, to come to her the Savior
    deigned,—
    He would not be, by her, in love outdone.
Gently He showed her then His blessed Face,
    And one word sprang from His deep Heart's
    recess:

Mary! His voice she knew, she knew its grace;
   It came with perfect peace her heart to bless.

One day, my God! I, too, like Magdalen,
   Desired to find Thee, to draw near to Thee;
So over earth's immense, wide-stretching plain,
   I sought its Master and its King to see.
Then cried I, though I saw the flowers bloom
   In beauty 'neath green trees and azure skies:
"O brilliant Nature! thou art one vast tomb,
   Unless God's Face shall greet my longing
   eyes."

A heart I need, to soothe me and to bless,—
   A strong support that can not pass away—
To love me wholly, e'en my feebleness,
   And never leave me through the night or day,
There is no one created thing below,
   Can love me truly, and can never die.
God become man—none else my needs can
   know;
   He, He alone, can understand my cry.

Thou comprehendest all I need, dear Lord!
   To win my heart, from heaven Thou didst
   come;
For me Thy blood didst shed, O King adored!
   And on our altars makest Thy home.
So, if I may not here behold Thy Face,

Or catch the heav'nly music of Thy Voice,
I still can live, each moment, by Thy grace,
    And in Thy Sacred Heart I can rejoice.

O Heart of Jesus, wealth of tenderness!
    My joy Thou art, in Thee I safely hide.
Thou, Who my earliest youth did charm and
    bless,
    Till my last evening, oh! with me abide,
All that I had, to Thee I wholly gave,
    To Thee each deep desire of mine is known.
Whoso his life shall lose, that life shall save—
    Let mine be ever lost in Thine alone!

I know it well—no righteousness of mine
    Has any value in Thy searching eyes;
Its every breath my heart must draw from
    Thine,
    To make of worth my life's long sacrifice.
Thou hast not found Thine angels without taint;
    Thy Law amid the thunderbolts was given;
And yet, my Jesus! I nor fear nor faint.
    For me, on Calvary, Thy Heart was riven.

To see Thee in Thy glory face to face—
    I know it well—the soul must pass through
    fires.
Choose I *on earth* my purgatorial place—
    The flaming love of Thy great Heart's desires!
So shall my exiled soul, to death's command,

Make answer with one cry of perfect love;
Then flying straight to heaven its Fatherland,
  Shall reach with no delay that home above.

October 1895

✺

"I THIRST FOR LOVE"

In wondrous love Thou didst come down from
  heaven
  To immolate Thyself, O Christ, for me;
So, in my turn, my love to Thee is given,
  I wish to suffer and to die for Thee.

Thou, Lord, hast spoken this truth benign;
  "To die for one loved tenderly
Of greatest love on earth is sign;"
  and now, such love is mine—
  such love for Thee!

Abide, abide with me, O Pilgrim blest!
  Behind the hill fast sinks the dying day.
Helped by Thy cross I mount the rocky crest;
  Oh, come, to guide me on my heavenward
  way.

To be like Thee is my desire;
Thy voice finds echo in my soul.
Suffering I crave! Thy words of fire

136

Lift me above earth's mire
And sin's control.

Chanting Thy victories, gloriously sublime,
The Seraphim—all heaven—cry to me,
That even Thou, to conquer sin and crime,
Upon this earth a sufferer must be.

For me, upon life's dreary way,
What scorn, what anguish, Thou didst bear
Let me grow humble every day,
Be least of all, always,
Thy lot to share!

Ah, Christ! Thy great example teaches me
Myself to humble, honors to despise.
Little and low like Thee I choose to be,
Forgetting self, so I may charm Thine eyes.

My peace I find in solitude,
Nor ask I more, dear Lord, than this:
Be my sole beatitude—
Ever, in Thee, renewed
My joy, my bliss!

Thou, the great God Whom earth and heaven
    adore,
Thou dwellest a prisoner for me night and day;
And every hour I hear Thy voice implore:
"I thirst—I thirst—I thirst—for love always!"

I, too, Thy prisoner am I;
I, too, cry ever unto Thee
Thine own divine and tender cry:
"I thirst! Oh, let me die
Of love for Thee!"

For love of Thee I thirst! Fulfill my hope;
Augment in me Thine own celestial flame!
For love of Thee I thirst! Too scant earth's scope.
The glorious Vision of Thy Face I claim!

My long slow martyrdom of fire
Still more and more consumes me.
Thou art my joy, my one desire.
Jesu! may I expire
Of love for Thee!

April 30, 1896

MY ARMOR
TO A NOVICE FOR HER PROFESSION DAY

"The spouse of the King is terrible as an army
    set in array; She is like to a choir of music on
    a field of battle" (cf. Song of Solomon 6:4).

"Put you on the armor of God that you may be
    able to stand against the deceits of the devil"
    (Ephesians 6:11).

With heavenly *armor* am I clad today;
    The hand of God has thus invested me.
What now from Him could tear my heart away;
    What henceforth come between my God and
    me?
With Him for Guide, the fight I face serene;
    Nor furious fire, nor foe, nor death, I fear.
My enemies shall know I am a queen,
    The spouse of God, most high, most dear.

This armor I shall keep while life shall last;
    Thou, Thou hast given it me, my King, my
    Spouse!
My fairest, brightest gems, by nothing on earth
    surpassed,
    Shall be my sacred vows.

My first dear sacrifice, O Poverty,
    You shall go with me till my dying hour.

Detached from all things must the athlete be,
   If he the race would run, and prove his power.

Taste, worldly men! regret, remorse and pain,
   The bitter fruits of earthly, vain desire;
The glorious palms of Poverty I gain,
   I who to God alone aspire.

"Who would My heavenly Kingdom have from
   Me,
   He must use violence," so Jesus said.
Ah well then! Poverty my mighty lance shall be,
   The *helmet* for my head.

The pure white Angels' sister now am I;
   My vow of *Chastity* has made me so.
Ah, how I hope one day with them to fly!
   Meanwhile to daily combat must I go
For my great Spouse, of every lord the Lord,
   Struggle must I, with neither truce nor rest;
And Chastity shall be my heavenly sword.
   To win men's souls to Jesus' breast.

Oh Chastity, my sword invincible!
   To overcome my foes thou hast sufficed;
By thee am I—O joy ineffable!—
   The Spouse of Jesus Christ.

The proud, proud angel, in the realms of light,
   Cried out, rebellious: "I will not obey!"

But I shall cry, throughout earth's dreary night,
  "With all my heart, I will obey always!"
With holy boldness all my soul is steeled,
  Against hell's wild attacks I bravely dart;
Obedience is my firm and mighty *shield*,
  The *buckler* on my valiant heart.

O conquering God! no other prize I seek,
  than to submit with all my heart to Thee;
Of victories the obedient man shall speak
  Through all eternity.
If now a soldier's weapon I can wield,
  If valiantly like him the foe I face,
I also long to sing upon the field,
  As sang the glorious Virgin of all grace.
You make the chords to vibrate on your lyre.
  That lyre, O Jesus! is my loving heart;
To sing Thy mercies is that heart's desire.
  How sweet, how strong, how dear, Thou art.

With radiant smile, dear Spouse, my heart's
  Delight,
  I go to meet all foes from hell's dark land;
And singing I shall die, upon the field of fight,
  My weapons in my hand.

                                        March 25, 1897

ABANDONMENT

Abandonment is the delicious fruit of love.

—St. Augustine

I saw upon this earth
   a marvelous tree arise;
Its vigorous root had birth,
   O wonder! in the skies.
Never, beneath its shade,
   Can aught disturb or wound;
There tempests are allayed,
   There perfect rest is found
And love men call this tree,
   From heaven's high portals sent;
Its fruit, how fair to see!
   Is named abandonment.

What banquet here does greet
   Each reverent, hungry guest!
How, by its odors sweet,
   The spirit is refreshed!
If we its fruit but touch,
   Joy seems on us to pour.
Oh, taste—for never such
   A feast was yours before.
In this tumultuous world
   It brings us perfect peace;
Though storms be round us hurled,
   Its quiet shall not cease.

Abandonment gives rest
  In Thee, O Jesus Christ!
Here is the food most blest
  That has Thy saints sufficed.
Spouse of my soul, draw nearer!
  I give my all to Thee.
What more can I desire
  Than Thy sweet Face to see?
Naught can I do but smile,
  Safe folded to Thy breast.
They who have known no guile
  Find there most perfect rest.

As looks the floweret small
  Up to the glorious sun,
So I, though least of all
  Seek my Beloved One.
King Whom I love the most!
  The star I always see
Is Thy White Sacred Host,
  Little and low like me;
And its celestial power,
  Down from Thine altar sent,
Wakes in my heart that flower—
  Perfect abandonment.

All creatures here below,
  At times, they weary me;
And willingly I go,

With God alone to be.
And if, sometimes, dear Lord,
  Of me Thou weariest,
I wait upon Thy word;
  Thy holy will is best.
Smiling, I wait in peace,
  Till Thou return to me;
And never shall they cease—
  My songs of love for Thee.

All pain I now despise,
  Naught can disquiet me;
Swifter than eagle flies,
  My spirit flies to Thee.
Beyond the gloomy cloud,
  Ever the skies are fair,
And angels sing aloud,
  And God is reigning there.
And yet without a tear
  I wait that bliss above,
Who in the Host have here
The perfect fruit of love.

May 1897

V

SPIRITUAL INFLUENCES
in the Life of
St. Thérèse

THE IMITATION OF CHRIST
BY THOMAS À KEMPIS

When Thérèse was still a girl at home, she became well acquainted with Thomas à Kempis's *The Imitation of Christ*. In fact, members of her family could begin reading any passage in the book, and Thérèse could finish reciting it from memory. At a time when Mass was sung or chanted in Latin, it's safe to say that à Kempis's classic work on Christian spirituality did more to form Thérèse's thoughts about faith than even her frequent attendance at church. While the liturgies created habits deep in the soul, where prayer happened and where both mind and emotion communed with the mysteries of faith, *The Imitation of Christ*, along with any other spiritual reading, gave young Thérèse words that she could interact with directly. It's difficult for readers today to relate to this unless they have experienced for themselves worship in languages they cannot understand well.

Thomas à Kempis (1380–1471) was born in Germany but did his schooling in the Netherlands, where he remained as a monastic. His authorship of *The Imitation of Christ* has been disputed at various times but is generally accepted today. This work has four parts: Book 1—Thoughts Helpful in the Life of the Soul; Book 2—The Interior Life; Book 3—Internal

Consolation; Book 4—An Invitation to Holy Communion.

One of the beauties of *The Imitation of Christ* is its simplicity and straightforward tone. It's not surprising that Thérèse, who considered herself "little"—or, childlike and simple in terms of spirituality—resonated with this book. And when we read this short passage, we see an accurate description of Thérèse:

> There are two wings that raise a man above earthly things—simplicity and purity. Simplicity must inspire his purpose, and purity his affection. Simplicity reaches out after God; purity discovers and enjoys him. No good deed will prove an obstacle to you if you are inwardly free from uncontrolled desires. And if you are free from uncontrolled desires, and seek nothing but the will of God and the good of your neighbor, you will enjoy this inner freedom. If your heart be right, then every created thing will become for you a mirror of life and a book of holy teaching. For there is nothing created so small and mean that it does not reflect the goodness of God.

ST. TERESA OF AVILA (1515–82)

Upon entering the Carmel at Lisieux, Thérèse inherited a rich tradition of prayer practices, from the chanted Divine Hours to solitary contemplation. She had St. Teresa of Avila to thank for that, in large part. It was St. Teresa who, three centuries earlier, had taken the Carmelite order back to its roots of simplicity, poverty, discipline, and prayer.

There are some interesting parallels and contrasts between the lives of these two women. Thérèse entered the Carmel at age fifteen, with her father's blessing and after an appeal to the pope. Teresa did not have her father's blessing; she ran away and joined the Carmelite convent at age twenty. Thérèse had no apparent interest in the opposite sex and marriage, whereas Teresa struggled with those temptations. Both women wrote their life stories and descriptions of their spiritual journeys by order of their superiors. And both entered mental, contemplative prayer naturally and could not resist this sort of relationship to the Divine.

In fact, St. Teresa is a great example of a person quite single-minded in relating to almighty God. Because she recognized that she was but a human being created to be in communion with the Creator, she approached God with a sort of fearlessness. Our Little Thérèse was just as fearless in that regard, clinging to God her Father and Jesus her Spouse with a relentless confidence. This passage from St. Teresa's *Way of Perfection* could have easily been written by Thérèse:

> Avoid being bashful with God, as some people are, in the belief that they are being humble. It would not be humility on your part if the King were to do you a favor and you refused to accept it; but you would be showing humility by taking it, and being pleased with it, yet realizing how far you are from deserving it. A fine humility it would be if I had the Emperor of heaven and earth in my house, coming to do me a favor and to delight in my company, and I were so humble that I would not answer his questions, nor remain with him, nor accept what he gave me, but left him alone. . . . Have nothing to do with that kind of humility, but speak with him as with a father, a brother, a Lord and a spouse—and, sometimes in one way and sometimes in another, he will teach you what you must do to please him. Do not be foolish; ask him to let you speak to him.

ST. JOHN OF THE CROSS (1542–91)

St. John of the Cross was a Carmelite friar, a contemporary of St. Teresa of Avila. His works would have been as familiar to the Carmelites at Lisieux as those of St. Teresa. Thérèse refers to his works numerous times in her autobiography.

At age twenty-one, John entered a Carmelite monastery in Medina, Spain. The Carmelites sent him to university, where he studied philosophy and theology and was ordained a priest. He later met the Carmelite reformer, Teresa of Avila, who was quick to recognize his spiritual aptitude. A friendship developed between them, and John became her partner in reform (as well as her spiritual director), helping to set up contemplative communities throughout the country.

Because reform is always a dangerous thing, and because John was such a force to be reckoned with—a gifted organizer, powerfully articulate, extremely popular with Christians whether lay or religious—he became a target of the Inquisition. He was imprisoned for several months during his thirties. Through mistreatment and deprivation he was pressured, without effect, to renounce his affiliation with Teresa. He not only survived the ordeal but during those dark days began composing in his head some of the poetry that would become the basis of his later writings.

The following stanza of St. John's poem, "Living Flame of Love," along with his own commentary upon it, gives us a stunning picture of the love Thérèse expressed in her life devoted to the Bridegroom Jesus.

Stanza 1

O living flame of love
That tenderly wounds my soul
In its deepest center! Since
Now you are not oppressive,
Now Consummate! if it be your will:
Tear through the veil of this sweet
  encounter.

This flame of love is the spirit of its bridegroom, which is the Holy Spirit. The soul feels him within itself not only as a fire which has consumed and transformed it, but as a fire that burns and flares within it. And that flame, every time it flares up, bathes the soul in glory and refreshes it with the quality of divine life. Such is the activity of the Holy Spirit in the soul transformed in love: the interior acts he produces shoot up flames, for they are acts of inflamed love in which the will of the soul united with that flame, made one with it, loves most sublimely.

THE GOSPELS

In her autobiography, Thérèse speaks quite plainly about the writings that have helped her:

How much enlightenment I have plumbed in the works of our father St. John of the Cross! At the age of seventeen and eighteen I had no other spiritual nourishment, but later all books left me in dryness, and I'm still in that state. If I open a book written by a spiritual author (even the most beautiful, the most touching), right away I feel my heart constrict, and I read, so to speak, without understanding, or if I understand, my mind stops without being able to meditate. In that state of impotence, Holy Scripture and the *Imitation of Christ* come to my aid. In them I find nourishment that is solid and completely pure. But above all it is the Gospels that keep me fed during my times of prayer. In them I find everything that is necessary to my poor little soul. In them I always discover new illuminations, hidden and mysterious meanings.

As Thérèse matured in her faith and neared the end of her short life, the words that most fed her soul and informed her thoughts were the Gospels. Although passages from both Old and New Testaments are quoted and/or cited frequently in her autobiography, her primary focus was on the life and words of Jesus. She took major themes from, for instance, his encounter with the Samaritan woman at the well. She absorbed with special attention his lengthy prayer for and about his disciples in John 14–17. She applied to herself the conversations of her Lord.

This emphasis upon the Gospels makes perfect sense in the life of the Little Flower. Her way to God was in the arms of Jesus, lifted up as a small child who could find no other means to reach perfection or saintliness. She spent hours in contemplation, allowing the Savior's words to come alive in her own heart. She moved through every day and each ordinary hour as one who walked at Jesus' side, in his constant company. And when in her own soul darkness descended, a long period during which she did not feel God's presence, her response was completely in tune with gospel grace:

> Above all I follow Magdalen, for the amazing, rather I should say, the loving audacity, that delights the Heart of Jesus, has cast its spell upon mine. It is not because I have been preserved from mortal sin that I lift up my heart to God in trust and love. I feel that even had I on my conscience every crime one could commit, I should lose nothing of my confidence: my heart broken with sorrow, I would throw myself into the Arms of my Saviour. I know that He loves the Prodigal Son. No one could frighten me, for I know what to believe concerning His Mercy and His love.

NOTES

All "Preparation" text was written by Vinita Hampton Wright.

All texts cited as "autobiography" are taken from one of four editions/translations of St. Thérèse of Lisieux's autobiography, most commonly known as *The Story of a Soul*. The edition used is indicated by the translator's last name—Beevers, Day, Edmonson, or Taylor. See the Bibliography for publication details.

I
THE PRAYER LIFE OF ST. THÉRÈSE OF LISIEUX

6   *O my God*   Autobiography, Taylor, 8–9.

14   *In Thérèse's time*   O'Donnell, *Prayer: Insights from St. Thérèse of Lisieux*, 42.

16   *I feel then that the fervor of my sisters*   O'Connor, *In Search of Therese*, 108.

I went to confession only a few times   O'Connor, *In Search of Therese*, 120.

21   *By 1905*   O'Connor, *Therese of Lisieux*, 146–147.

II
PRAYING ALONGSIDE ST. THÉRÈSE

33   *I'm suffering very much*   Clarke, *St. Therese of Lisieux: Her Last Conversations*. Translation of the "Yellow Notebook" of Mother Agnes, August 18, entry #1, 152.

34   *We who run*   Clarke, Yellow Notebook, July 23, #3.

35   *Since my First Communion*   Clarke, Yellow Notebook, July 31, #13.

III
THE DAILY OFFICE FOR SUNDAY THROUGH SATURDAY

43   *How sweet is the way of love!*   Autobiography, Beevers, 108.

47   *May I recall*   Venerable Mother Therese of Saint Augustine, quoted in Hickey, *Bread of Heaven: A Treasury of Carmelite Prayers and Devotions on the Eucharist*, 61.

     O Jesus! thou Sun   Gueranger, *The Liturgical Year, Passiontide and Holy Week*, early Lenten hymn, 28.

49   *He shall gather*   Autobiography, Day, 192–93.

50   *I confess to almighty God*   Gueranger, *The Liturgical Year, Passiontide and Holy Week*, morning prayer, 29.

52   *In order that my life*   Autobiography, Taylor, 195.

53   *O God! who has enlightened*   Gueranger, *The Liturgical Year, Christmas*, night prayer, 45.

54   *I used to go into a space*   Autobiography, Beevers, 39–40.

58   *How good and how sweet it is*   Bernard of Clairvaux, quoted in *The Book of Catholic Prayer*, 574.

59   *O God, who makes the souls of the faithful*   Collect, fourth Sunday after Easter, *Roman Missal*, adapted.

60   *For me, prayer is an upward*   Autobiography, Edmonson, 274.

61   *O my God, I am exceedingly grieved*   Gueranger, *The Liturgical Year, Passiontide and Holy Week*, night prayer, Act of Contrition, 33.

64 *Come, adore this wondrous presence*   St. Thomas Aquinas, quoted in Storey, *A Catholic Book of Hours and Other Devotions*, 156.

   O almighty and everlasting God   Gueranger, *The Liturgical Year, Time after Pentecost*, night prayer, 21.

65 *A heart given to God*   Autobiography, Day, 149.

69 *O true Lord and my Glory!*   St. Teresa of Avila, quoted in Beasley-Topliffe, *The Soul's Passion for God: Selected Writings of Teresa of Avila*, 25.

70 *O God who has prepared for them*   Collect, fifth Sunday after Pentecost, *Roman Missal*, adapted.

71 *What would happen if*   Autobiography, Edmonson, 124.

72 *Almighty and most merciful God*   Collect, for Sorrow for Sin, *Roman Missal*, 1418.

75 *Blessed Jesus, still my soul in you*   St. John of the Cross, quoted in *John of the Cross: Selections from The Dark Night and Other Writings*, 113.

   O God, who made blessed John   Collect dedicated to St. John of the Cross, *Roman Missal*, 1217.

76 *Protect, O Lord, thy people*   Gueranger, *The Liturgical Year, Christmas*, night prayer, Prayer for the Saints' Intercession, 42.

77 *I'm suffering only for an instant*   Clarke, Yellow Notebook, August 19, #10.

82 *O almighty God, seeing that amid so many*   Collect, Monday of Holy Week, *Roman Missal*, adapted.

   Mercifully consider our weakness   Collect, for a Martyr Bishop, *Roman Missal*.

83   *God forgive me, but He knows*   Autobiography, Day, 146.

84   *O God, who shows the light of your truth*   Collect, third Sunday after Easter, *Roman Missal*, adapted.

86   *My God, here I am all devoted to Thee*   Brother Lawrence, *The Practice of the Presence of God*, Fourth Letter, 15.

       O God, who in thy wonderful providence Gueranger, *The Liturgical Year, Passiontide and Holy Week*, night prayer, 35.

87   *How happy God makes me!*   Autobiography, Beevers, 147.

93   *O God, who has honored the Order of Carmel* Collect dedicated to the Carmelite Order.

       O God, our refuge and strength   Collect, twenty-second Sunday after Pentecost, *Roman Missal,* adapted.

94   *If you find me dead one morning*   Clarke, Yellow Notebook, June 5, #4.

95   *Almighty, everlasting God, who in the abundance* Collect, eleventh Sunday after Pentecost, *Roman Missal*, adapted.

97   *God our Father, source of all holiness*   November 1, *Roman Missal.*

98   *Visit, we beseech thee, O Lord, this house and family* Gueranger, *The Liturgical Year, Passiontide and Holy Week*, night prayer, 37.

99   *If all the weak and imperfect souls*   Autobiography, Edmonson, 209.

103   *O Brightness of the Father's glory*   Gueranger, *The Liturgical Year, Time after Pentecost*, morning prayer, 14–15.

104   *You know my weakness, Lord*   Kane, *The Prayers of Saint Therese of Lisieux*, 116.

105   *Even if I had accomplished all the works*   Clarke, Yellow Notebook, June 23.

106   *O almighty and most merciful God, who didst draw from a rock*   Collect, prayer for sorrow for sin, *Roman Missal*, 1418.

108   *May you be blessed forever!*   St. Teresa of Avila, *Life*, 6:9.

109   *Graciously hear us, O God our Savior*   Collect dedicated to St. Teresa of Avila, *Roman Missal*, 1170, adapted.

      God our Father, you have promised   Opening prayer for Thérèse's feast day Mass, *Roman Missal*.

110   *So you see, Mother, what a very little soul I am!*   Autobiography, Day, 181.

115   *O eternal God, Turn us into the arms and hands*   Hildegard of Bingen, quoted in *2000 Years of Prayer*, 122.

      My God, I offer you all that I do   Kane, *The Prayers of Saint Therese of Lisieux*, 86.

116   *It's not Martha's works that Jesus blamed*   Autobiography, Edmonson, 295.

117   *O Jesus! how happy I would be if I had been faithful*   Kane, *The Prayers of Saint Therese of Lisieux*, 75.

120   *God be in my head, And in my understanding*   Sarum Primer, quoted in *The Book of Catholic Prayer*, 296.

IV. PRAYERS AND POEMS OF ST. THÉRÈSE

All poems in this section are from *Poems of St. Teresa, Carmelite of Lisieux, known as the "Little Flower of Jesus"* by St. Therese of Lisieux, trans. S.L. Emery, 1907. Available through Christian Classics Ethereal Library, Grand Rapids, MI.

All prayers in this section are from *Story of a Soul (L'Histoire d'une Ame): The Autobiography of St. Therese of Lisieux* by St. Therese of Lisieux. London, 1912. Available through Christian Classics Ethereal Library, Grand Rapids, MI.

V. SPIRITUAL INFLUENCES
IN THE LIFE OF ST. THÉRÈSE

BIBLIOGRAPHY

2000 Years of Prayer. Compiled by Michael Counsell. Harrisburg, PA: Morehouse Publishing, 1999.

The Book of Catholic Prayer. Compiled by Sean Finnegan. Chicago: Loyola Press, 2000.

Bread of Heaven: A Treasury of Carmelite Prayers and Devotions on the Eucharist. Compiled by Penny Hickey. Notre Dame, IN: Christian Classics, 2006.

A Catholic Book of Hours and Other Devotions. Edited by William G. Storey. Chicago: Loyola Press, 2007.

Gueranger, Prosper. *The Liturgical Year*. London, 1867. Reprinted by The Newman Press, Westminster, MD, 1949.

John of the Cross: Selections from The Dark Night and Other Writings. Edited by Emilie Griffin. San Francisco: HarperSanFrancisco, 1987.

The Lion Christian Meditation Collection. Compiled by Hanna Ward and Jennifer Wild. Oxford, England: Lion Publishing, 1998.

The Mass Every Day of the Year: The Roman Missal. Translated by Edward A. Pace and John J. Wynne. New York: Home Press, 1916.

O'Connor, Patricia. *In Search of Therese*. Wilmington, DE: Michael Glazier, 1987.

O'Connor, Patricia. *Therese of Lisieux: A Biography.* Huntington, IN: Our Sunday Visitor, 1983.

O'Donnell, Christopher. *Prayer: Insights from St. Thérèse of Lisieux.* Dublin, Ireland: Veritas Publications, 2001.

The Prayers of Saint Therese of Lisieux. Translated by Aletheia Kane. Washington, DC: ICS Publications, 1997.

The Roman Missal in Latin and English for Every Day in the Year. Dublin, Ireland: M. H. Gill & Son, 1948.

The Soul's Passion for God: Selected Writings of Teresa of Avila. Selected, edited, and introduced by Keith Beasley-Topliffe. Nashville: Upper Room Books, 1997.

St. Therese of Lisieux: Her Last Conversations. Translated by John Clarke. Washington, DC: ICS Publications, 1973.

The Story of a Soul: The Autobiography of Saint Therese of Lisieux. Translated by John Beevers. New York: Doubleday/Image Books, 2001.

The Story of a Soul: The Autobiography of Saint Therese of Lisieux. Translated by Michael Day. Rockford, IL: Tan Books & Publishers, 1951.

Story of a Soul (L'Histoire d'une Ame) : The Autobiography of St. Therese of Lisieux. Edited by T.N. Taylor. London, 1912. Available through Christian Classics Ethereal Library, Grand Rapids, MI.

The Story of a Soul: St. Thérèse of Lisieux. Translated by Robert J. Edmonson. Brewster, MA: Paraclete Press, 2006.

INDEX OF SUBJECTS

INDEX OF SCRIPTURES

Note: Page numbers are in parentheses. Scripture books/chapters are in bold.

INDEX OF AUTHORS AND SOURCES

ABOUT PARACLETE PRESS

WHO WE ARE

Paraclete Press is a publisher of books, recordings, and DVDs on Christian spirituality. Our publishing represents a full expression of Christian belief and practice—from Catholic to Evangelical, from Protestant to Orthodox.

We are the publishing arm of the Community of Jesus, an ecumenical monastic community in the Benedictine tradition. As such, we are uniquely positioned in the marketplace without connection to a large corporation and with informal relationships to many branches and denominations of faith.

WHAT WE ARE DOING

PARACLETE PRESS BOOKS | Paraclete publishes books that show the richness and depth of what it means to be Christian. Although Benedictine spirituality is at the heart of all that we do, we publish books that reflect the Christian experience across many cultures, time periods, and houses of worship. We publish books that nourish the vibrant life of the church and its people.

We have several different series, including the best-selling Paraclete Essentials and Paraclete Giants series of classic texts in contemporary English; Voices from the Monastery—men and women monastics writing about living a spiritual life today; award-winning poetry; best-selling gift books for children on the occasions of baptism and first communion; and the Active Prayer Series that brings creativity and liveliness to any life of prayer.

MOUNT TABOR BOOKS | Paraclete's newest series, Mount Tabor Books, focuses on liturgical worship, art and art history, ecumenism, and the first millennium church; and was created in conjunction with the Mount Tabor Ecumenical Centre for Art and Spirituality in Barga, Italy.

PARACLETE RECORDINGS | From Gregorian chant to contemporary American choral works, our recordings celebrate the best of sacred choral music composed through the centuries that create a space for heaven and earth to intersect. Paraclete Recordings is the record label representing the internationally acclaimed choir Gloriæ Dei Cantores, praised for their "rapt and fathomless spiritual intensity" by *American Record Guide*; the Gloriæ Dei Cantores Schola, specializing in the study and performance of Gregorian chant; and the other instrumental artists of the Gloriæ Dei Artes Foundation.

Paraclete Press is also privileged to be the exclusive North American distributor of the recordings of the Monastic Choir of St. Peter's Abbey in Solesmes, France, long considered to be a leading authority on Gregorian chant.

PARACLETE VIDEO | Our DVDs offer spiritual help, healing, and biblical guidance for a broad range of life issues including grief and loss, marriage, forgiveness, facing death, bullying, addictions, Alzheimer's, and spiritual formation.

Learn more about us at our website:
www.paracletepress.com or phone us
toll-free at 1.800.451.5006

SCAN
TO
READ
MORE

Popular Guides to Prayer

The St. Francis Prayer Book

ISBN: 978-1-55725-352-1
$16.99, French flaps

This warm-hearted little book is a window into the soul of St. Francis, one of the most passionate and inspiring followers of Jesus.

• Pray the words that Francis taught his spiritual brothers and sisters to pray.
• Explore Francis's time and place and feel the joy and earnestness of the first Franciscans.
• Experience how it is possible to live a contemplative and active life, at the same time.

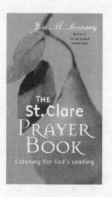

The St. Clare Prayer Book

ISBN: 978-1-55725-513-6
$16.99, Paperback

Discover the spirituality of St. Clare and how it complements that of St. Francis. Enter into a week of morning and evening prayer centered on themes from Clare's life. Pray with Clare's own words in a variety of occasions.